Is Multiculturalism
Bad for Women?

Is Multiculturalism Bad for Women?

SUSAN MOLLER OKIN

WITH RESPONDENTS

EDITED BY JOSHUA COHEN,
MATTHEW HOWARD,
AND MARTHA C. NUSSBAUM

PRINCETON UNIVERSITY PRESS, PRINCETON, NEW JERSEY

Copyright © 1999 by Princeton University Press
Published by Princeton University Press, 41 William Street,
Princeton, New Jersey 08540
In the United Kingdom: Princeton University Press,
Chichester, West Sussex

Library of Congress Cataloging-in-Publication Data

Okin, Susan Moller.
Is multiculturalism bad for women? / Susan Moller Okin
with respondents ; edited by Joshua Cohen, Matthew Howard,
and Martha C. Nussbaum.
p.   cm.
Includes bibliographical references.
ISBN 0-691-00431-5 (cloth : alk. paper). —
ISBN 0-691-00432-3 (pbk. : alk. paper)
1. Minority women—Social conditions. 2. Sex discrimination
against women. 3. Multiculturalism. 4. Culture conflict.
5. Feminism. I. Cohen, Joshua, 1951–   . II. Howard, Matthew, 1971–
III. Nussbaum, Martha Craven, 1947–   . IV. Title.
HQ1161.045   1999
305.42—dc21   99-21303

This book has been composed in Sabon

The paper used in this publication meets
the minimum requirements of
ANSI/NISO Z39.48-1992 (R1997)
(*Permanence of Paper*)

http://pup.princeton.edu

Printed in the United States of America

1   3   5   7   9   10   8   6   4   2

5   7   9   10   8   6
(PBK.)

CONTENTS

✳

CONTENTS

*Is Multiculturalism
Bad for Women?*

Introduction
Feminism, Multiculturalism, and Human Equality

JOSHUA COHEN,

MATTHEW HOWARD, AND

MARTHA C. NUSSBAUM

Over the past two centuries, social and political hierarchies in this country have met with repeated challenge from movements inspired by ideas of human equality. Abolitionists insisted that slaves are human beings, not to be held as property. Working-class movements of the 1920s and 1930s argued that a decent life for human beings should not depend on market success. The civil rights struggle of the 1960s said that skin color must be irrelevant to human fate, and condemned the practice of racial apartheid. More recently, movements for gay and lesbian rights have rejected the idea that people should be subjected to public humiliation for their choice of sexual partner.

Similarly with the modern women's movement and the feminist theory associated with it. That movement condemned settled practice—stunning levels of violence against women, ceaseless efforts to turn women's sexuality into a special burden, and persistent disparities of economic opportunity—in the name of the radical idea that women are human beings, too; that they are the moral equals of men, owed equal respect and concern, and that women's lives are not to be discounted nor women to be treated as a subordinate caste.

Over the past decade, a variety of movements, theories, and proposals have emerged under the banner of "multiculturalism." Though some embrace a romantic politics of group identity, others

3

make a straightforward egalitarian claim. Multiculturalism, according to one especially compelling formulation, is the radical idea that people in other cultures, foreign and domestic, are human beings, too—moral equals, entitled to equal respect and concern, not to be discounted or treated as a subordinate caste. Thus understood, multiculturalism condemns intolerance of other ways of life, finds the human in what might seem Other, and encourages cultural diversity.

But on closer inspection, multiculturalism resists easy reconciliation with egalitarian convictions. After all, some cultures do not accept, even as theory, the principle that people are owed equal respect and concern (of course, no culture fully practices the principle). Moreover, tensions with decent treatment for women seem especially acute. In some contemporary cultures we see practices—including differential nutrition and health care, unequal rights of ownership, assembly, and political participation, unequal vulnerability to violence, and the denial of educational opportunities—that appear to fly in the face of the idea that women are entitled to be treated as equals. Such tensions become especially clear when we consider a controversial proposal endorsed by some multiculturalists: to provide cultural minorities with "group rights" as a way to preserve those minorities from undue pressure on their ways of life. But how can we endorse special rights for groups that treat female members as subordinate no-counts?

Susan Okin, a leading political theorist, forcefully puts that question to us in the lead essay in this volume. Okin's essay, originally published in *Boston Review*, observes that regnant cultural ideas—including religious ideas—sometimes provide rationales for controlling women's bodies and ruling their lives. When the dominant ideas and practices in a group offend so deeply against the idea that men and women are moral equals, Okin argues, we ought to be less solicitous of the group and more attentive to the costs visited on female members.

The responses to Okin's essay—many of which appeared in an earlier form in *Boston Review*—range widely. Some emphasize more than Okin does the plasticity of cultures and religions, and conclude (with Okin) that they can fairly be expected to adapt to minimal demands of political morality—for example, that women are to be treated as equals. Some broadly agree with Okin, but suggest that her focus on women's status is arbitrary: Shouldn't we condemn group rights *whenever* a culture is unduly constraining of its members? Others think it intolerant to require that cultures and religious outlooks endorse, in theory or practice, the egalitarian principle, and to condition special rights on such endorsement. A final group thinks that Okin's juxtaposition of feminism and multiculturalism is blind to cultural differences—a failing rooted ultimately in her confusion (characteristic of moral universalists) of the generically human with its familiar, local visage.

The exploration of these disagreements sharply clarifies the central question in this debate: How should we understand a commitment to equality in a world of multiple human differences, grim hierarchies of power, and cruel divisions of life circumstance? And at its best moments, the debate pushes beyond such clarification, forcing us to rethink our understanding of feminism and multiculturalism, and to reflect on the practical prospects for reconciling these different aspects of the radical idea of human equality—to consider how we might achieve, in Susan Okin's words, "a multiculturalism that effectively treats all persons as each other's moral equals."

PART 1

Is Multiculturalism Bad for Women?

*

SUSAN MOLLER OKIN

U NTIL THE past few decades, minority groups—immigrants as well as indigenous peoples—were typically expected to assimilate into majority cultures. This assimilationist expectation is now often considered oppressive, and many Western countries are seeking to devise new policies that are more responsive to persistent cultural differences. The appropriate policies vary with context: countries such as England, with established churches or state-supported religious education, find it difficult to resist demands to extend state support to minority religious schools; countries such as France, with traditions of strictly secular public education, struggle over whether the clothing required by minority religions may be worn in the public schools. But one issue recurs across all contexts, though it has gone virtually unnoticed in current debate: what should be done when the claims of minority cultures or religions clash with the norm of gender equality that is at least formally endorsed by liberal states (however much they continue to violate it in their practices)?

In the late 1980s, for example, a sharp public controversy erupted in France about whether Magrébin girls could attend school wearing the traditional Muslim head scarves regarded as proper attire for postpubescent young women. Staunch defenders of secular education lined up with some feminists and far-right nationalists against the practice; much of the Old Left supported the multiculturalist demands for flexibility and respect for diversity, accusing opponents of racism or cultural imperialism. At the very same time, however, the public was virtually silent about a problem of vastly greater importance to many French Arab and African immigrant women: polygamy.

During the 1980s, the French government quietly permitted immigrant men to bring multiple wives into the country, to the point where an estimated 200,000 families in Paris are now polygamous. Any suspicion that official concern over head scarves was motivated by an impulse toward gender equality is belied by the easy adoption of a permissive policy on polygamy, despite the burdens this practice imposes on women and the warnings disseminated by women from the relevant cultures.[1] On this issue, no politically effective opposition galvanized. But once reporters finally got around to interviewing the wives, they discovered what the government could have learned years earlier: that the women affected by polygamy regarded it as an inescapable and barely tolerable institution in their African countries of origin, and an unbearable imposition in the French context. Overcrowded apartments and the lack of private space for each wife led to immense hostility, resentment, even violence both among the wives and against each other's children.

In part because of the strain on the welfare system caused by families with twenty to thirty members, the French government has recently decided to recognize only one wife and to consider all the other marriages annulled. But what will happen to all the other wives and children? Having ignored women's views on polygamy for so long, the government now seems to be abdicating its responsibility for the vulnerability that its rash policy has inflicted on women and children.

The French accommodation of polygamy illustrates a deep and growing tension between feminism and multiculturalist concern for protecting cultural diversity. I think we—especially those of us who consider ourselves politically progressive and opposed to all forms of oppression—have been too quick to assume that feminism and multiculturalism are both good things which are easily reconciled. I shall argue instead that there is considerable likelihood of tension between them—more precisely, between feminism and a multiculturalist commitment to group rights for minority cultures.

A few words to explain the terms and focus of my argument. By *feminism*, I mean the belief that women should not be disadvantaged by their sex, that they should be recognized as having human dignity equal to that of men, and that they should have the opportunity to live as fulfilling and as freely chosen lives as men can. *Multiculturalism* is harder to pin down, but the particular aspect that concerns me here is the claim, made in the context of basically liberal democracies, that minority cultures or ways of life are not sufficiently protected by the practice of ensuring the individual rights of their members, and as a consequence these should also be protected through special *group* rights or privileges. In the French case, for example, the right to contract polygamous marriages clearly constituted a group right not available to the rest of the population. In other cases, groups have claimed rights to govern themselves, to have guaranteed political representation, or to be exempt from certain generally applicable laws.

Demands for such group rights are growing—from indigenous native populations, minority ethnic or religious groups, and formerly colonized peoples (at least when the latter immigrate to the former colonial state). These groups, it is argued, have their own "societal cultures" which—as Will Kymlicka, the foremost contemporary defender of cultural group rights, says—provide "members with meaningful ways of life across the full range of human activities, including social, educational, religious, recreational, and economic life, encompassing both public and private spheres."[2] Because societal cultures play so pervasive and fundamental a role in the lives of their members, and because such cultures are threatened with extinction, minority cultures should be protected by special rights. That, in essence, is the case for group rights.

Some proponents of group rights argue that even cultures that "flout the rights of [their individual members] in a liberal society"[3] should be accorded group rights or privileges if their minority status endangers the culture's continued existence. Others do not claim that all minority cultural groups should have special rights, but rather that such groups—even illiberal ones that violate their individual members' rights, requiring them to conform to group beliefs or norms—have the right to be "left alone" in a liberal society.[4] Both claims seem clearly inconsistent with the basic liberal value of individual freedom, which entails that group rights should not trump the individual rights of its members; thus I will not address the additional problems they present for feminists here.[5] But some defenders of multiculturalism confine their defense of group rights largely to groups that are internally liberal.[6] Even with these restrictions, feminists—everyone, that is, who endorses the moral equality of men and women—should remain skeptical. So I will argue.

11

Gender and Culture

Most cultures are suffused with practices and ideologies concerning gender. Suppose, then, that a culture endorses and facilitates the control of men over women in various ways (even if informally, in the private sphere of domestic life). Suppose, too, that there are fairly clear disparities in power between the sexes, such that the more powerful, male members are those who are generally in a position to determine and articulate the group's beliefs, practices, and interests. Under such conditions, group rights are potentially, and in many cases actually, antifeminist. They substantially limit the capacities of women and girls of that culture to live with human dignity equal to that of men and boys, and to live as freely chosen lives as they can.

Advocates of group rights for minorities within liberal states have not adequately addressed this simple critique of group rights, for at least two reasons. First, they tend to treat cultural groups as monoliths—to pay more attention to differences between and among groups than to differences within them. Specifically, they accord little or no recognition to the fact that minority cultural groups, like the societies in which they exist (though to a greater or lesser extent), are themselves *gendered*, with substantial differences in power and advantage between men and women. Second, advocates of group rights pay little or no attention to the private sphere. Some of the most persuasive liberal defenses of group rights urge that individuals need "a culture of their own," and that only within such a culture can people develop a sense of self-esteem or self-respect, as well as the capacity to decide what kind of life is good for them. But such arguments typically neglect both the different roles that cultural groups impose on their members and the context in which persons' senses of themselves and their capacities are first formed *and* in which culture is first transmitted—the realm of domestic or family life.

When we correct for these deficiencies by paying attention to internal differences and to the private arena, two particularly important connections between culture and gender come into sharp relief, both of which underscore the force of this simple critique of group rights. First, the sphere of personal, sexual, and reproductive

life functions as a central focus of most cultures, a dominant theme
in cultural practices and rules. Religious or cultural groups often are
particularly concerned with "personal law"—the laws of marriage,
divorce, child custody, division and control of family property, and
inheritance.[7] As a rule, then, the defense of "cultural practices" is
likely to have much greater impact on the lives of women and girls
than on those of men and boys, since far more of women's time and
energy goes into preserving and maintaining the personal, familial,
and reproductive side of life. Obviously, culture is not only about
domestic arrangements, but they do provide a major focus of most
contemporary cultures. Home is, after all, where much of culture is
practiced, preserved, and transmitted to the young. On the other
hand, the distribution of responsibilities and power at home has a
major impact on who can participate in and influence the more public parts of the cultural life, where rules and regulations about both
public and private life are made. The more a culture requires or
expects of women in the domestic sphere, the less opportunity they
have of achieving equality with men in either sphere.

The second important connection between culture and gender is
that most cultures have as one of their principal aims the control of
women by men.[8] Consider, for example, the founding myths of
Greek and Roman antiquity, and of Judaism, Christianity, and
Islam: they are rife with attempts to justify the control and subordination of women. These myths consist of a combination of denials
of women's role in reproduction; appropriations by men of the
power to reproduce themselves; characterizations of women as
overly emotional, untrustworthy, evil, or sexually dangerous; and
refusals to acknowledge mothers' rights over the disposition of their
children.[9] Think of Athena, sprung from the head of Zeus, and of
Romulus and Remus, reared without a human mother. Or Adam,
made by a male God, who then (at least according to one of the
two biblical versions of the story) created Eve out of part of Adam.
Consider Eve, whose weakness led Adam astray. Think of all those
endless "begats" in Genesis, where women's primary role in reproduction is completely ignored, or of the textual justifications for
polygamy, once practiced in Judaism, still practiced in many parts
of the Islamic world and (though illegally) by Mormons in some

parts of the United States. Consider, too, the story of Abraham, a pivotal turning point in the development of monotheism.[10] God commands Abraham to sacrifice "his" beloved son. Abraham prepares to do exactly what God asks of him, without even telling, much less asking, Isaac's mother, Sarah. Abraham's absolute obedience to God makes him the central, fundamental model of faith for all three religions.

Although the powerful drive to control women—and to blame and punish them for men's difficulty in controlling their own sexual impulses—has been softened considerably in the more progressive, reformed versions of Judaism, Christianity, and Islam, it remains strong in their more orthodox or fundamentalist versions. Moreover, it is by no means confined to Western or monotheistic cultures. Many of the world's traditions and cultures, including those practiced within formerly conquered or colonized nation-states—which certainly encompasses most of the peoples of Africa, the Middle East, Latin America, and Asia—are quite distinctly patriarchal. They too have elaborate patterns of socialization, rituals, matrimonial customs, and other cultural practices (including systems of property ownership and control of resources) aimed at bringing women's sexuality and reproductive capabilities under men's control. Many such practices make it virtually impossible for women to choose to live independently of men, to be celibate or lesbian, or to decide not to have children.

Those who practice some of the most controversial of such customs—clitoridectomy, polygamy, the marriage of children or marriages that are otherwise coerced—sometimes explicitly defend them as necessary for controlling women and openly acknowledge that the customs persist at men's insistence. In an interview with *New York Times* reporter Celia Dugger, practitioners of clitoridectomy in Côte d'Ivoire and Togo explained that the practice "helps insure a girl's virginity before marriage and fidelity afterward by reducing sex to a marital obligation." As a female exciser said, "[a] woman's role in life is to care for her children, keep house and cook. If she has not been cut, [she] might think about her own sexual pleasure."[11] In Egypt, where a law banning female genital cutting was recently overturned by a court, supporters of the practice say it "curbs a girl's sexual appetite and makes her more marriageable."[12] Moreover, in such societies, many women have no economically viable alternative to marriage.

In polygamous cultures, too, men readily acknowledge that the practice accords with their self-interest and is a means of controlling women. As a French immigrant from Mali said in a recent interview: "When my wife is sick and I don't have another, who will care for me? . . . [O]ne wife on her own is trouble. When there are several, they are forced to be polite and well behaved. If they misbehave, you threaten that you'll take another wife." Women apparently see polygamy very differently. French African immigrant women deny that they like polygamy and say that not only are they given "no choice" in the matter, but their female forebears in Africa did not like it either.[13] As for child or otherwise coerced marriage: this practice is clearly a way not only of controlling who the girls or young women marry but also of ensuring that they are virgins at the time of marriage and, often, of enhancing the husband's power by creating a significant age difference between husbands and wives.

Consider, too, the practice—common in much of Latin America, rural Southeast Asia and parts of West Africa—of pressuring or even requiring a rape victim to marry the rapist. In many such cultures—including fourteen countries in Central and South America—rapists are legally exonerated if they marry or (in some cases) simply offer to marry their victims. Clearly, rape is not seen in these cultures primarily as a violent assault on the girl or woman herself but rather as a serious injury to her family and its honor. By marrying his victim, the rapist can help restore the family's honor and relieve it of a daughter who, as "damaged goods," has become unmarriageable. In Peru, this barbaric law was amended for the worse in 1991: the codefendants in a gang rape now are all exonerated if just one of them offers to marry the victim (feminists are fighting to get the law repealed). As a Peruvian taxi driver explained: "Marriage is the right and proper thing to do after a rape. A raped woman is a used item. No one wants her. At least with this law the woman will get a husband."[14] It is difficult to imagine a worse fate for a woman than being pressured into marrying the man who has raped her. But worse fates do exist in some cultures—notably in Pakistan and parts of the Arab Middle East, where women who bring rape charges quite frequently are charged themselves with the serious Muslim offense of *zina*, or sex outside of marriage. Law allows for the whipping or imprisonment of such women, and culture condones the killing or pressuring into suicide of a raped woman by relatives intent on restoring the family's honor.[15]

Thus many culturally based customs aim to control women and render them, especially sexually and reproductively, servile to men's desires and interests. Sometimes, moreover, "culture" or "traditions" are so closely linked with the control of women that they are virtually equated. In a recent news report about a small community of Orthodox Jews living in the mountains of Yemen, the elderly leader of this small polygamous sect is quoted as saying: "We are Orthodox Jews, very keen on our traditions. If we go to Israel, we will lose hold over our daughters, our wives and our sisters." One of his sons added, "We are like Muslims, we do not allow our women to uncover their faces."[16] Thus the servitude of women is presented as virtually synonymous with "our traditions." (Ironically, from a feminist point of view, the story was entitled "Yemen's Small Jewish Community Thrives on Mixed Traditions." Only blindness to sexual servitude can explain the title; it is inconceivable that the article would have carried such a title if it were about a community that practiced any kind of slavery but sexual slavery.)

While virtually all of the world's cultures have distinctly patriarchal pasts, some—mostly, though by no means exclusively, Western liberal cultures—have departed far further from them than others. Western cultures, of course, still practice many forms of sex discrimination. They place far more importance on beauty, thinness, and youth in females and on intellectual accomplishment, skill, and strength in males. They expect women to perform for no economic reward far more than half of the unpaid work related to home and family, whether or not they also work for wages; partly as a consequence of this and partly because of workplace discrimination, women are far more likely than men to become poor. Girls and women are also subjected by men to a great deal of (illegal) violence, including sexual violence. But women in more liberal cultures are, at the same time, legally guaranteed many of the same freedoms and opportunities as men. In addition, most families in such cultures, with the exception of some religious fundamentalists, do not communicate to their daughters that they are of less value than boys, that their lives are to be confined to domesticity and service to men and children, and that their sexuality is of value only in marriage, in the service of men, and for reproductive ends. This situation, as we have seen, is quite different from that of women in many of the world's other cultures, including many of those from which immigrants to Europe and North America come.

GROUP RIGHTS?

Most cultures are patriarchal, then, and many (though not all) of the cultural minorities that claim group rights are more patriarchal than the surrounding cultures. So it is no surprise that the cultural importance of maintaining control over women shouts out to us in the examples given in the literature on cultural diversity and group rights within liberal states. Yet, though it shouts out, it is seldom explicitly addressed.[17]

A paper by Sebastian Poulter about the legal rights and culture-based claims of various immigrant groups and Gypsies in contemporary Britain mentions the roles and status of women as "one very clear example" of the "clash of cultures."[18] In it, Poulter discusses claims put forward by members of such groups for special legal treatment on account of their cultural differences. A few are non–gender-related claims; for example, a Muslim schoolteacher's being allowed to be absent part of Friday afternoons in order to pray, and Gypsy children's being subject to less stringent schooling requirements than others on account of their itinerant lifestyle. But the vast majority of the examples concern gender inequalities: child marriages, forced marriages, divorce systems biased against women, polygamy, and clitoridectomy. Almost all of the legal cases discussed by Poulter stemmed from women's or girls' claims that their individual rights were being truncated or violated by the practices of their own cultural groups. In a recent article by political philosopher Amy Gutmann, fully half her examples have to do with gender issues—polygamy, abortion, sexual harassment, clitoridectomy, and purdah.[19]

This is quite typical in the literature on subnational multicultural issues. Moreover, the same linkage between culture and gender occurs in practice in the international arena, where women's human rights are often rejected by the leaders of countries or groups of countries as incompatible with their various cultures.[20]

Similarly, the overwhelming majority of "cultural defenses" that are increasingly being invoked in U.S. criminal cases involving members of cultural minorities are connected with gender—in particular with male control over women and children.[21] Occasionally, cultural defenses are cited in explanation of expectable violence among men or the ritual sacrifice of animals. Much more common, however, is the argument that, in the defendant's cultural group, women are not human beings of equal worth but rather subordinates whose primary (if not only) function is to serve men sexually and domestically. Indeed, the four types of cases in which cultural defenses have been used most successfully are: (1) kidnap and rape by Hmong men who claim that their actions are part of their cultural practice of *zij poj niam*, or "marriage by capture"; (2) wife-murder by immigrants from Asian and Middle Eastern countries whose wives have either committed adultery or treated their husbands in a servile way; (3) murder of children by Japanese or Chinese mothers who have also tried but failed to kill themselves, and who claim that because of their cultural backgrounds the shame of their husbands' infidelity drove them to the culturally condoned practice of mother-child suicide; and (4) in France—though not yet in the United States, in part because the practice was criminalized only in 1996—clitoridectomy. In a number of such cases, expert testimony about the accused's or defendant's cultural background has resulted in dropped or reduced charges, culturally based assessments of *mens rea*, or significantly reduced sentences. In a well-known recent case in the United States, an immigrant from rural Iraq married his two daughters, aged 13 and 14, to two of his friends, aged 28 and 34. Subsequently, when the older daughter ran away with her 20-year-old boyfriend, the father sought the help of the police in finding her. When they located her, they charged the father with child abuse and the two husbands and boyfriend with statutory rape. The Iraqis' defense is based in part on their cultural marriage practices.[22]

As the four examples show, the defendants are not always male, nor the victims always female. Both a Chinese immigrant man in New York who battered his wife to death for committing adultery and a Japanese immigrant woman in California who drowned her children and tried to drown herself because her husband's adultery had shamed the family relied on cultural defenses to win reduced charges (from first-degree murder to second-degree murder or involuntary manslaughter). It might seem, then, that the cultural defense was biased toward the male in the first case and the female in the second. But though defendants of different sexes were cited, in both cases, the cultural message is similarly gender-biased: women (and children, in the second case) are ancillary to men and should bear the blame and the shame for any departure from monogamy. Whoever is guilty of the infidelity, the wife suffers: in the first case, by being brutally killed on account of her husband's rage at her shameful infidelity; in the second, by being so shamed and branded such a failure by his infidelity that she is driven to kill herself and her children. Again, the idea that girls and women are first and foremost sexual servants of men—that their virginity before marriage and fidelity within it are their preeminent virtues—emerges in many of the statements made in defense of cultural practices.

Western majority cultures, largely at the urging of feminists, have recently made substantial efforts to preclude or limit excuses for brutalizing women. Well within living memory, American men were routinely held less accountable for killing their wives if they explained their conduct as a crime of passion, driven as they were by jealousy and rage over the wife's infidelity. Also not long ago, female rape victims who did not have completely celibate pasts or who did not struggle—even when to do so meant endangering themselves—were routinely blamed for the attack. Things have now changed to some extent, and doubts about the turn toward cultural defenses undoubtedly are prompted in part by a concern to preserve recent advances. Another concern is that such defenses can distort perceptions of minority cultures by drawing excessive attention to negative aspects of them. But perhaps the primary concern is that, by failing to protect women and sometimes children of minority cultures from male and sometimes maternal violence, cultural defenses violate women's and children's rights to equal protection of the laws.[23] When a woman from a more patriarchal culture comes to the United States (or some other Western, basically liberal, state), why should she be less protected from male violence than other women are? Many women from minority cultures have protested the double standard that is being applied on behalf of their aggressors.[24]

LIBERAL DEFENSE

Despite all this evidence of cultural practices that control and subordinate women, none of the prominent defenders of multicultural group rights has adequately or even directly addressed the troubling connections between gender and culture or the conflicts that arise so commonly between feminism and multiculturalism. Will Kymlicka's discussion is, in this respect, representative.

Kymlicka's arguments for group rights are based on the rights of individuals and confine such privileges and protection to cultural groups that are internally liberal. Following John Rawls, Kymlicka emphasizes the fundamental importance of self-respect in a person's life. He argues that membership in a "rich and secure cultural structure,"[25] with its own language and history, is essential both for the development of self-respect and for giving persons a context in which they can develop the capacity to make choices about how to lead their lives. Cultural minorities need special rights, then, because their cultures may otherwise be threatened with extinction, and cultural extinction would be likely to undermine the self-respect and freedom of group members. Special rights, in short, put minorities on an equal footing with the majority.

The value of freedom plays an important role in Kymlicka's argument. As a result, except in rare circumstances of cultural vulnerability, a group that claims special rights must govern itself by recognizably liberal principles, neither infringing on the basic liberties of its own members by placing internal restrictions on them nor discriminating among them on grounds of sex, race, or sexual preference.[26] This requirement is of great importance to a consistently liberal justification of group rights, because a "closed" or discriminatory culture cannot provide the context for individual development that liberalism requires, and because otherwise collective rights might result in subcultures of oppression within and facilitated by liberal societies. As Kymlicka says, "To inhibit people from questioning their inherited social roles can condemn them to unsatisfying, even oppressive lives."[27]

As Kymlicka acknowledges, this requirement of internal liberalism rules out the justification of group rights for the "many fundamentalists of all political and religious stripes who think that the best community is one in which all but their preferred religious, sexual, or aesthetic practices are outlawed." For the promotion and support of *these* cultures undermines "the very reason we had for being concerned with cultural membership—that it allows for meaningful individual choice."[28] But the examples I cited earlier suggest that far fewer minority cultures than Kymlicka seems to think will be able to claim group rights under his liberal justification. Though they may not impose their beliefs or practices on others, and though they may appear to respect the basic civil and political liberties of women and girls, many cultures do not, especially in the private sphere, treat them with anything like the same concern and respect with which men and boys are treated, or allow them to enjoy the same freedoms. Discrimination against and control of the freedom of females are practiced, to a greater or lesser extent, by virtually all cultures, past and present, but especially by religious ones and those that look to the past—to ancient texts or revered traditions—for guidelines or rules about how to live in the contemporary world. Sometimes more patriarchal minority cultures exist in the midst of less patriarchal majority cultures; sometimes the reverse is true. In either case, the degree to which each culture is patriarchal and its willingness to become less so should be crucial factors in judgment about the justifications of group rights—once women's equality is taken seriously.

Clearly, Kymlicka regards cultures that discriminate overtly and formally against women—by denying them education or the right to vote or hold office—as not deserving special rights.[29] But sex discrimination is often far less overt. In many cultures, strict control of women is enforced in the private sphere by the authority of either actual or symbolic fathers, often acting through, or with the complicity of, the older women of the culture. In many cultures in which women's basic civil rights and liberties are formally assured, discrimination practiced against women and girls within the household not only severely constrains their choices but also seriously threatens their well-being and even their lives.[30] And such sex discrimination—whether severe or more mild—often has very powerful *cultural* roots.

Although Kymlicka rightly objects, then, to the granting of group rights to minority cultures that practice overt sex discrimination, his arguments for multiculturalism fail to register what he acknowledges elsewhere: that the subordination of women is often informal and private, and that virtually no culture in the world today, minority or majority, could pass his "no sex discrimination" test if it were applied in the private sphere.[31] Those who defend group rights on liberal grounds need to address these very private, culturally reinforced kinds of discrimination. For surely self-respect and self-esteem require more than simple membership in a viable culture. Surely it is *not* enough for one to be able to "question one's inherited social roles" and to have the capacity to make choices about the life one wants to lead, that one's culture be protected. At least as important to the development of self-respect and self-esteem is *our place within our culture.* And at least as pertinent to our capacity to question our social roles is *whether our culture instills in us and forces on us particular social roles*. To the extent that a girl's culture is patriarchal, in both these respects her healthy development is endangered.

PART OF THE SOLUTION?

It is by no means clear, then, from a feminist point of view, that minority group rights are "part of the solution." They may well exacerbate the problem. In the case of a more patriarchal minority culture in the context of a less patriarchal majority culture, no argument can be made on the basis of self-respect or freedom that the female members of the culture have a clear interest in its preservation. Indeed, they *might* be much better off if the culture into which they were born were either to become extinct (so that its members would become integrated into the less sexist surrounding culture) or, preferably, to be encouraged to alter itself so as to reinforce the equality of women—at least to the degree to which this value is upheld in the majority culture. Other considerations would, of course, need to be taken into account, such as whether the minority group speaks a language that requires protection, and whether the group suffers from prejudices such as racial discrimination. But it would take significant factors weighing in the other direction to counterbalance evidence that a culture severely constrains women's choices or otherwise undermines their well-being.

What some of the examples discussed above illustrate is how culturally endorsed practices that are oppressive to women can often remain hidden in the private or domestic sphere. In the Iraqi child marriage case mentioned above, if the father himself had not called in agents of the state, his daughters' plight might well not have become public. And when Congress in 1996 passed a law criminalizing clitoridectomy, a number of U.S. doctors objected to the law on the basis that it concerned a private matter which, as one said, "should be decided by a physician, the family, and the child."[32] It can take more or less extraordinary circumstances for such abuses of girls or women to become public or for the state to be able to intervene protectively.

Thus it is clear that many instances of private-sphere discrimination against women on cultural grounds are never likely to emerge in public, where courts can enforce the women's rights and political theorists can label such practices as illiberal and therefore unjustified violations of women's physical or mental integrity. Establishing group rights to enable some minority cultures to preserve themselves may not be in the best interests of the girls and women of those cultures, even if it benefits the men.

Those who make liberal arguments for the rights of groups, then, must take special care to look at inequalities within those groups. It is especially important to consider inequalities between the sexes, since they are likely to be less public, and thus less easily discernible. Moreover, policies designed to respond to the needs and claims of cultural minority groups must take seriously the urgency of adequately representing less powerful members of such groups. Because attention to the rights of minority cultural groups, if it is to be consistent with the fundamentals of liberalism, must ultimately be aimed at furthering the well-being of the members of these groups, there can be no justification for assuming that the groups' self-proclaimed leaders—invariably composed mainly of their older and their male members—represent the interests of all of the groups' members. Unless women—and, more specifically, young women (since older women often are co-opted into reinforcing gender inequality)—are fully represented in negotiations about group rights, their interests may be harmed rather than promoted by the granting of such rights.

d/n
provide
way for
this
Phillips does

PART 2

Responses

*

Whose Culture?

KATHA POLLITT

*

SUSAN OKIN writes that multiculturalism and feminism are in "tension," and sometimes even in opposition to each other. She argues that defenders of "cultural" or "group rights" for minority cultures have failed to notice that there are considerable differences of power within those cultures, and that those differences are gendered, with men having power over women. She also claims that group-rights advocates fail to pay enough attention to the private, domestic sphere, in which these oppressive and gendered cultural traditions tend to be most freely exercised.

Coming in late to this debate, I have to say I've had a hard time understanding how anyone could find these arguments controversial. Feminism and multiculturalism may find themselves allied in academic politics, where white women and minority women and men face common enemies (Great Books, dead white men, old boy networks, job discrimination, and so forth). But as political visions in the larger world they are very far apart. In its demand for equality for women, feminism sets itself in opposition to virtually every culture on earth. You could say that multiculturalism demands respect for all cultural traditions, while feminism interrogates and challenges all cultural traditions. Feminists might disagree about strategic issues: what needs changing first, or how to ensure one isn't just making things worse, or how to win over enough people. Feminists might even disagree about what true equality is in a given instance. But fundamentally, the ethical claims of feminism run counter to the cultural relativism of "group rights" multiculturalism.

Okin notes that the flashpoints for cultural rights tend to be around issues of gender, a.k.a. "the family," and she cites a number of prominent legal cases in which immigrants have put forward cultural defenses against charges of wife murder, child murder, the forced marriage of underage daughters to strangers, clitoridectomy, and so forth. (She might have included the role that multicultural arguments play in cases involving the harsh disciplining of children, homophobia, and sex education.) Although she herself sets aside, as clearly unmeritorious, the notion of "group rights" for immigrants, who have, after all, made a decision to come here, these cases raise interesting questions: What is a culture, and how do you know? A Chinese immigrant murders his supposedly unfaithful wife and says this is the way they do things back home. Many were outraged, and rightly so, that this multicultural equivalent of the Twinkie Defense was successful as a legal strategy. Not so many paused to wonder whether the defense argument was based on fact. Is it really legal in modern China for husbands to murder their wives if they think their wives are having affairs? China has undergone a great deal of social change in the twentieth century—change that includes dramatic, if uneven, gains in rights for women. Maybe in China lots of husbands kill their wives; maybe, as in the United States, such men are motivated by tacit cultural values (men who can't control their wives are impotent wimps, crimes of passion aren't so bad, etc.), but this is a different story from the one told by the defendant's lawyer, which portrayed him as the naive product of a rigid, static society who somehow found himself living in New York City and who could not be expected to adapt.

True or (in my view) false, you'll note that this is not an argument that just any immigrant can make. A Russian, an Italian, could not justify beating his wife to death by referring to the customs of dear old Moscow or Calabria, although Russian women are killed by their male partners at astronomical rates and parts of Italy are very old-fashioned indeed about these matters. That is partly because of multiculturalism's connections to Third Worldism, and the appeals Third Worldism makes to white liberal guilt, and partly because Americans understand that Russia and Italy are dynamic societies in which change is constant and interests clash. The cultural rights argument works best for cultures that most Americans know comparatively little about: cultures that in our ignorance we can imagine as stable, timeless, ancient, lacking in internal conflict, premodern. But where on the globe today is such a society? Even the supposedly ancient traditions defended by group-rights advocates sometimes turn out to be of rather recent vintage. Clitoridectomy, it's worth remembering, was falling into desuetude in Kenya when nationalists revived it as part of their rejection of British colonialism. Israeli family law, which is extremely unfair to women—divorce is unilateral for men only, for example, as under Islamic law—is the result of a political deal between the religious and secular Zionists who founded the state.

That cultural-rights movements have centered on gender is a telling fact about them. It's related to the way in which nationalism tends to identify the nation with the bodies of its women: they are the ones urged into "traditional" dress, conceptualized as the producers of babies for the fatherland and keepers of the hearth for the men at the front, punished for sleeping with outsiders, raped by the nation's enemies, and so forth. But it's also partly due to the fact that gender and family are retrograde areas of most majority cultures, too: these are accommodations majority cultures have often been willing to make. How far would an Algerian immigrant get, I wonder, if he refused to pay the interest on his Visa bill on the grounds that Islam forbids interest on borrowed money? Or a Russian who argued that the cradle-to-grave social security provided by the former Soviet Union was part of his cultural tradition and should be extended to him in Brooklyn as well? Everyone understands that money is much too important to be handed out in this whimsical fashion. Women and children are another story.

An older friend of mine was in Paris while the dispute over Muslim schoolgirls' head scarves was going on. A gentle, tolerant, worldly-wise leftist, she sided with the girls against the government: why shouldn't they be able to dress as they wished, to follow their culture? Then she came across a television debate in which a Muslim girl said she wanted the ban to stay because without it, her family would force her to wear a scarf. That changed my friend's view of the matter: the left, and feminist, position, she now thought, was to support this girl and the ones like her in their struggle to be independent modern women—not the parents, the neighbors, the community and religious "leaders." I think my friend was right.

Liberal Complacencies

WILL KYMLICKA

✳

I AGREE with the basic claim of Okin's paper—that a liberal egalitarian (and feminist) approach to multiculturalism must look carefully at intragroup inequalities, and specifically at gender inequalities, when examining the legitimacy of minority group rights. Justice within ethnocultural groups is as important as justice between ethnocultural groups. Group rights are permissible if they help promote justice between ethnocultural groups, but are impermissible if they create or exacerbate gender inequalities within the group.

In my recent work, I have tried to emphasize this point by distinguishing between two kinds of "group rights." Sometimes an ethnocultural group claims rights against its own members—in particular, the right to restrict individual choice in the name of cultural "tradition" or cultural "integrity." I call such group rights "internal restrictions," since their aim is to restrict the ability of individuals within the group (particularly women) to question, revise, or abandon traditional cultural roles and practices. A liberal theory of minority group rights, I have argued, cannot accept such internal restrictions, since they violate the autonomy of individuals and create injustice within the group.

However, liberals can accept a second sort of group rights—namely, rights that a minority group claims against the larger society in order to reduce its vulnerability to the economic or political power of the larger society. Such rights, which I call "external protections," can take the form of language rights, guaranteed political representation, funding of ethnic media, land claims, compensation for historical injustice, or the regional devolution of power. All of these can help to promote justice between ethnocultural groups, by ensuring that members of the minority have the same effective capacity to promote their interests as the majority.

Okin argues, in effect, that my account of "internal restrictions" is too narrow. I defined internal restrictions as those claims by a group which involve limiting the civil and political liberties of individual members, but Okin insists that the ability of women to question and revise their traditional gender roles can be drastically curtailed even when their civil rights are formally protected in the public sphere.

I accept this point. In fact, I had not intended "individual freedoms" to be interpreted in a purely formal or legalistic way, and I would consider the domestic oppressions that Okin discusses to be paradigmatic examples of the sorts of "internal restrictions" which liberals must oppose.

So I accept Okin's claim that we need a more subtle account of internal restrictions which helps us identify limitations on the freedom of women within ethnocultural groups. But it still seems to me that the basic distinction is sound—i.e., liberals can accept external protections which promote justice between groups, but must reject internal restrictions which reduce freedom within groups. Okin is suggesting a constructive elaboration of this distinction, but I see no reason to reject the underlying principle.

Yet Okin seems to think that feminists should therefore be deeply skeptical about the very category of minority group rights. More generally, she suggests that feminists should view multiculturalism not as a likely ally in a broader struggle for a more inclusive justice, but as a likely threat to whatever gains feminists have made over the last few decades.

I think this way of opposing feminism and multiculturalism is regrettable. After all, both are making the same point about the inadequacy of the traditional liberal conception of individual rights. In her own work, Okin has argued that women's equality cannot be achieved solely through women's being given the same set of formal individual rights which men possess. We must also pay attention to the structure of societal institutions (e.g., the workplace, family, etc.), and to the sorts of images and expectations people are exposed to in schools and the media, since these are typically gendered in an unfair way, using the male as the "norm."

Similarly, multiculturalists argue that we cannot achieve justice between ethnocultural groups simply by guaranteeing to ethnocultural minorities the same set of formal individual rights which the majority possesses. We must also examine the structure of institutions (e.g., the language, calendar, and uniforms that they use), and the content of schooling and media, since all of these take the majority culture as the "norm."

Moreover, both feminists and multiculturalists provide the same explanation for why traditional liberal theories are not satisfactory. Historically, liberal theorists were explicitly prejudiced against women and ethnic or racial minorities. Today, however, the problem is one of invisibility. In her work, Okin has shown how liberal theorists implicitly or explicitly operate with the assumption that the citizen is a man, and never ask what sorts of institutions or principles women would choose (e.g., if they were behind Rawls's "veil of ignorance"). In my work, I show that liberal theorists have operated with the assumption that citizens share the same language and national culture, and never ask what sorts of institutions would be chosen by ethnocultural minorities. In both cases, the distinctive needs and interests of women and ethnocultural minorities are simply never addressed in the theory. And in both cases, the result is that liberalism has been blind to grave injustices which limit the freedom and harm the self-respect of women and ethnocultural minorities.

Finally, both feminism and multiculturalism look to similar remedies. Okin says that she is concerned about the view that the members of a minority "are not sufficiently protected by the practice of ensuring the individual rights of their members," and minority group members are demanding "a group right not available to the rest of the population." But many feminists have made precisely the same argument about gender equality—i.e., that true equality will require rights for women that are not available to men, such as affirmative action, women-only classrooms, gender-specific prohibitions on pornography, gender-specific health programs, and the like. Others have made similar arguments about the need for group-specific rights and benefits for the disabled, or for gays and lesbians. All of these movements are challenging the traditional liberal assumption that equality requires identical treatment.

So I see multiculturalism and feminism as allies engaged in related struggles for a more inclusive conception of justice. Indeed, my own thoughts on ethnocultural justice have been deeply influenced by Okin's work on gender justice, since I think there are many comparable historical patterns and contemporary lessons.

Okin worries that the currently fashionable attention to multiculturalism is obscuring the older struggle for gender inequality. This is true of some multiculturalists, just as it is true that some feminists have been blind to issues of cultural difference. But it would be a mistake—in both theory and practice—to think that struggling against gender inequality within ethnocultural groups requires denying or downplaying the extent of injustice between groups. These are both grave injustices, and liberalism's historic inability to recognize them is rooted in similar theoretical mistakes. The same attitudes and habits of mind that enabled liberals to ignore the just claims of women have also enabled them to ignore the just claims of ethnocultural minorities. We have a common interest in fighting these liberal complacencies.

"My Culture Made Me Do It"

BONNIE HONIG

*

MOVING quickly from veiling to polygamy to efforts to control female sexuality to the denial of maternal rights over children to the (paradoxically contradictory) enforcement of maternalism as women's proper role to clitoridectomy to child marriage to forced marriage to one's rapist to marriage by capture and, finally, to murder, Susan Okin asks whether groups that are illiberal and sexist should be accorded group rights and protections by liberal states, or whether, instead, sexist cultural practices and perhaps entire cultures should be altered or allowed to become "extinct." Okin implies that the slope from veiling to murder is slippery and that everything from veiling to murder is an expression of just one essential thing: male violence against women. Denuding veiling, polygamy, clitoridectomy of all their context, signification, and meaning, Okin sees such practices merely as symptoms of patriarchal projects that aim to clothe female abjection in the increasingly socially and politically acceptable guise of "culture."

Okin is quite right to worry that the fragile gains of feminism may be attenuated by heightened multicultural sensitivities. After struggling for so long to increase gender equality in hiring, wages, and promotions, and to decrease violence against women, feminists really ought to be concerned that their newly gained ground (such as it is) might be lost by way of what starts out as concessions to "difference" (so-called). It is not at all counterintuitive to think that in a few years' time, group rights that are tensely related to women's human rights may get extended not only to national minorities (as Kymlicka would like) and immigrant groups and ethnic groups, but also to cultural and religious groups until virtually all of the population is covered in one way or another by some cultural exemption. At the same time, however, feminists ought to be careful lest they participate in the recent rise of nationalist xenophobia by projecting a rightly feared backlash—whose proponents are mostly native-born Americans—onto foreigners who come from somewhere else and bring their foreign, (supposedly) "backward" cultures with them.

Okin is right, too, to insist that "when a woman from a more patriarchal culture comes to the United States (or some other Western, basically liberal, state)," she should be no "less protected from male violence than other women are." But this claim does not preclude our taking into account (without blindly accepting) the perspectives of new immigrants when passing judgment on their illegal acts. More to the point, Okin's claim about women's fight for equal protection from male violence begs the deeper questions of what constitutes male violence, and what counts as sex inequality, and what exactly "culture" and its extinction have to do with either of these things.

"Culture" has been used as an excuse for cruelty and violations of human rights by members of minority cultures in the United States as well as by states like China. When men or states claim that "my culture made me do it," they are claiming a kind of privacy or privilege that must surely be resisted for the sake of both human rights and "culture": neither is well served by it. Women's rights are human rights, and they must be protected as such from systemic violence as well as from idiosyncratic harm. And, contra Okin, culture is something rather more complicated than patriarchal permission for powerful men to subordinate vulnerable women. There are brutal men (and women) everywhere. Is it their Jewish, Christian, or Muslim identity that makes them brutal . . . or is it their brutality?

Rather than vigorously interrogate the spurious excuse "my culture made me do it," Okin accepts the claim—she sees the misogynist actions she's addressing as symptomatic of the ("foreign") cultures to which the actors are connected—and so she comes, unsurprisingly, to the conclusion that feminism demands that we get rid of the offending cultures or aid their transformation into more familiar sexual and familial practices. But the cultures Okin mentions are less univocally patriarchal than she suggests. And the unfamiliar practices she labels sexist are more complicated and ambiguous than that label allows. These limits of Okin's approach are evident in her reading of the three major religions:

1. Contra Okin, Judaism, Christianity and Islam do not just seek to "control" women's sexuality. Such efforts are usually matched by efforts to control male sexuality as well. While little room is provided for women to live "independently" from men (nuns are a stunning exception to this claim), equally little room is provided for men to live independently from women.

2. One can see Judaism as a series of erasures of maternal ties (as Okin suggests by way of the numerous patrilineal "begats" of the Hebrew Bible) but to do so one has to overlook the fact that Judaism itself (as opposed to its biblical tribal ties) is passed on matrilineally.

3. Athena, and Romulus and Remus, may exemplify a tendency among the ancients to explore the idea of nonmaternal birth. But the virgin birth of Jesus just as surely attenuates the role of the father in reproduction (as Dan Quayle might well have pointed out a few years back).

4. Veiling might be a sign of sexist, enforced female subservience, as Okin claims with reference to Yemenite Jews. Or it can be one part of a broader complex of efforts aimed at both sexes in order to manage a community's sexual and other relations. We need to know something about how veiling functions, what it signifies, in a particular context before we can decide that it means for everyone what it means for us. Like Okin, the secularist Left in France saw veiling as an affront to enlightened sex equality (as practiced in France?). But many Muslim feminists (they do exist but are obscured by Okin's liberal feminist lens, through which liberal brands of equality and individualism are equated to feminism) see veiling as an empowering practice. Veiling allows upwardly mobile professional women to move from the familiar settings of their rural homes and "emerge socially into a sexually integrated" urban world that is "still an alien, uncomfortable social reality for both women and men," says Leila Ahmed.[1]

5. One can see polygamy, permitted by premodern Judaism and contemporary Islam and once required by Mormonism, as a device

whereby men control women. There is surely no shortage of boastful men like the one Okin quotes: "[O]ne wife on her own is trouble. When there are several, they are forced to be polite and well behaved. If they misbehave, you threaten that you'll take another wife." But polygamy may not always serve the husband's interests so well. As the same newspaper article goes on to report, the three wives of another immigrant to France banded together when he married a fourth and prepared to bring his young bride home from Dakar. " 'They say if the new one comes, they will all leave, " Mr. Diop said. With three wives in France and one in Dakar, Mr. Diop said he has great prestige in his village, but he is unsure how to deal with the rebellion at home." In this instance, the institution of polygamy put women in a situation of solidarity. By contrast, the institution of monogamy, which Okin presents as unambiguously preferable to polygamy from a feminist perspective, famously isolates women from each other and privatizes them. The struggles of monogamous wives against their husbands' power are small, individual rebellions, usually unsupported these days by any networks of belonging. Surely monogamy, every man's little dominion, is no less often turned into an instrument of male power than is polygamy.

Obviously, these brief examples—drawn from a single newspaper article—cannot settle a debate about whether monogamy or polygamy better positions women to be empowered agents in relation to men, but they usefully complicate the easy judgment that either institution is better or worse as such, and they invite us to defamiliarize our own institutional arrangements and reflect more critically upon them. In particular, we might well ask why liberal states should be in the business of regulating sexuality at all. And we might also usefully wonder whether liberalism and feminism are themselves necessarily completely compatible, as Okin seems to think.

Okin assumes that Western liberal regimes are simply and plainly "less patriarchal" than other regimes, rather than differently so, perhaps worse in some respects and better in others. Her faith that Western liberal regimes have advanced furthest along a progressive trajectory of unfolding liberal equality prevents her from engaging in a more selective and comparative analysis of particular practices, powers, and contexts that could well enlighten us about ourselves

and heighten our critical awareness of some of the limits, as well as
the benefits, of liberal ways of life. For example, liberalism's commitment to individual rights has definitely improved the lot of many
women by positioning the state to protect them when necessary. But
liberalism's relentless individualism also feeds a privatizing, with-
drawalist conception of citizenship that is at least tensely related to
feminism's project of empowering women to act in concert to advance their own aims. If there is a question to be posed about
whether feminism is well served by multiculturalism—and there
surely is—there is just as surely a question to be posed about
whether feminism is entirely well served by its association with liberalism. Perhaps the partnership of liberalism and feminism is more
agonistic than Okin allows.

Moreover, an analysis of the tense relations between feminism and
multiculturalism must be careful not to conflate different with "culture" and "culture" with foreignness. Okin mentions, to great effect, the case of "an immigrant from rural Iraq [who] married his
two daughters, aged 13 and 14, to two of his friends, aged 28 and
34." Arrested for his actions, the father explained that such arrangements are quite ordinary in his native village. Okin treats the father's
actions as symptomatic of his particular "foreign" biases and values.
Perhaps the mere mention of Jerry Lee Lewis's famous (but not unusual) marriage some years ago to his 13-year-old cousin will suffice
to remind us that such practices are not exactly unheard-of in the
United States. Indeed, Lewis was no less surprised than was Okin's
Iraqi to find that marriage to such a young bride was controversial.

"Culture" is a way of life, a rich and timeworn grammar of
human activity, a set of diverse and often conflicting narratives
whereby communal (mis)understandings, roles, and responsibilities
are negotiated. As such, "culture" is a living, breathing system for
the distribution and enactment of agency, power, and privilege
among its members and beyond. Rarely are those privileges distrib-
uted along a single axis of difference such that, for example, all men
are more powerful than all women. Race, class, locality, lineage all
accord measures of privilege or stigma to their bearers. However,
even those who are least empowered in a certain setting have some
measure of agency in that setting, and their agency is bound up with

(though not determined by) the cultures, institutions, and practices that gave rise to it. Thus, extinguishing cultures is not the answer. In any case, years of colonial and assimilationist experiments should have taught us by now that such efforts are ethically problematic as well as self-defeating in practice.

Okin's other alternative—supporting a culture's own efforts "to alter itself so as to reinforce the equality," rather than the inequality, of women—is much more promising and is, indeed, already being pursued by feminists such as Leila Ahmed and Rey Chow, and by groups such as Women Living Under Islamic Law. But the promise of this approach depends in part upon the willingness of Western feminists to hold their own practices up to the same critical scrutiny they apply to Others, to hear the plural voices of women everywhere and to learn from them, while also refusing to prejudge the merits of practices that are unfamiliar or threatening to those of us raised in bourgeois liberal societies. For the sake of a future solidarity of women as feminists, the question of what constitutes gender (in)-equality must be kept disturbingly open to perpetual reinterroga-tion. (This openness *is* disturbing: clitoridectomy has its female de-fenders as well, a phenomenon explored in Nuruddin Farah's novel *Sardines*.) And we must all resist the all-too-familiar and dangerous temptation to mark foreignness itself as fundamentally threatening to women.

Is Western Patriarchal Feminism Good for Third World / Minority Women?

AZIZAH Y. AL-HIBRI

*

THE ISSUE of conflicting rights raised by Susan Okin's paper is of fundamental importance to any serious human rights discourse. Okin's perspective, discussion, and proposal, however, all suffer from three fatal problems: (1) stereotypical views of the "Other"; (2) a conflation of distinct belief systems; and (3) conflict with American constitutional principles.

The paper is clearly written from the perspective of the dominant cultural "I," a Western point of view burdened with immigrant problems and the human rights conflicts they engender. Okin blames this conflict on a Western liberal tradition that recognizes value in the very existence of cultural diversity.[1] She argues that some cultures may in fact be worthy of extinction.[2]

Okin's statement is remarkable in its honesty. If she is right about the universality of her principles, then, of course, why should women from other cultures have a lower standard of human rights crafted especially for them? In fact, whether immigrants or residents in their home country, why should women wait for salvation, when the West can readily defend their rights by use of force if necessary? Certainly, Okin's position has more integrity than one which views the "natives" or "alien immigrants" condescendingly and argues, under the guise of Western liberalism, that "those people" should be allowed to live in accordance with their own lower standards of human rights.

Luckily, these two options are not exhaustive. To recognize other alternatives, we need to revisit Okin's article and uncover its first fatal error. A quick look at her endnotes reveals what was already obvious to a culturally sensitive reader: her understanding of other cultures/religions is derived from secondary sources outside these cultures/religions. As a result, Okin commits simple but significant factual errors in assessing other belief systems. She argues, for example, that "the founding myths" of Judaism, Christianity, and Islam "are rife with attempts to justify the control and subordination of women" and, among other things, characterize women as "overly emotional, untrustworthy, evil, or sexually dangerous."[3] As proof, she offers two stories: the creation of Eve out of part of Adam and the fall of Adam.

But the Qur'an nowhere says that Eve was created out of part of Adam. In fact, the Qur'an clearly states that males and females were created by God from the same *nafs* (soul or spirit), and that the most honored among them in the sight of God is the most pious.[4] The story of the fall of Adam is also different in the Qur'an. *Both* Adam *and* Eve were tempted by Satan, and both succumbed.[5] The story is thus about the human condition. It is not about gender. By missing these important differences, Okin attributes to Islam a position based on biblical analysis. This is a serious form of religious reductionism. It is also the example par excellence of Okin speaking in her dominant voice about the *inessential Other.* So inessential is this Other that, even when included in the discussion, it is rendered remarkably indistinguishable and voiceless. It is allowed into the discussion only through the voice and perceptions of the dominant "I." Given these ground rules, it is hard to have a serious discussion or reach a democratic resolution of existing conflicts.

The importance of a genuine dialogue is that it permits a more accurate diagnosis of the problems at hand. While "founding myths" are not patriarchal in Islam, several jurists have succeeded in developing a patriarchal interpretation of various Qur'anic passages.[6] It is these passages with the related jurisprudence, and not the "founding myths," that need to be addressed in Islam. Unfortunately, an Orientalist reductionist approach to Islam often delays productive dialogue.[7]

I now turn to the second fatal error in Okin's piece: her conflation of distinct systems of belief. In attempting to refute the thesis that minority cultures should be protected by special rights, Okin draws many of her examples from the domain of religious belief. From the outset, she refers to such matters as Muslim head scarves, polygamy, and early marriages.[8] In later passages, Okin moves from culture to religion, as if they were interchangeable. From the outside, they may very well be. From the inside, the distinction amounts to the difference between acceptance and rejection of change.

To put this complicated issue in its proper perspective, we need to know a few basic Islamic principles. First, Islamic society is based on a system of *shura* (consultation) and the individual right to *ijtihad* (jurisprudential interpretation of religious text); hence there is no central authority charged with the task of interpreting the religion to the faithful.[9] As a result, women, as much as men, are entitled to engage in *ijtihad* (and have).[10] And each Muslim, male or female, is guaranteed his or her freedom of conscience.[11] Second, Islam was revealed as a world religion and thus, according to Qur'anic verse, celebrates diversity.[12] For this reason, a Muslim country may retain all local customs not inconsistent with Islamic revelation.[13] As a result of this principle, many countries retained local customs that we find controversial, and that have been erroneously viewed in the West, and sometimes locally, as Islamic. Third, Islamic jurisprudence adopts the principle that many laws change with the change of time and place, yet many Muslims continue to follow the jurisprudence of past centuries and civilizations. Finally, Muslim jurists believe that the laws of the Wise Lawgiver serve human *maslaha* (public interest).

A true feminist call to reform in Muslim countries or among Muslim immigrants must respect their religious and cultural sentiments, while recognizing the sanctity of the first and flexibility of the second. This means that with respect to issues such as those raised by Okin, the better approach is for Muslim feminists to reexamine existing Islamic jurisprudence critically in light of established jurisprudential principles and the *maslaha* of the Muslims. The result is a tripartite strategy. First, clearly separate customary from religious practices. This would significantly reduce the resistance of Muslims to certain types of change—namely, purely cultural changes. Second, reexamine existing jurisprudence critically to reveal any inappropriate cultural elements in it. Third, provide modern contributions to Islamic jurisprudence, which take into account the time, place, and *maslaha* of Muslims, half of whom are women. Such a complicated and time-consuming project cannot be truncated or canceled owing to the impatience of secular feminists.

This leads to the third fatal error in Okin's discussion: it conflicts with American constitutional principles that we value greatly, such as the separation of church and state and the freedom of belief. It may not be immediately clear that the separation issue is involved, precisely because Okin conflated religious and cultural issues. Once the distinction is drawn, it becomes clear that, at least in this country, people of faith are entitled to their religious beliefs whether secular feminists approve of these beliefs or not. This principle is at the heart of our democracy. Its violation can lead only to oppression through denial of basic civil rights.

Okin casts the conflict as one in which feminists and human rights advocates are attempting to save the women of minority cultures from internal oppression. Framed this way, the endeavor is admirable. Different accounts, however, reveal different scenarios. For example, many contemporary women with established careers have adopted the Orthodox or Hasidic Jewish way of life as adults.[14] This way of life includes, among other things, early marriages, gender roles, praying behind a *mechitzah* (partition separating men from women), and even *mikvah* (ritual bath) ceremonies (following menstruation).[15] It is hard for Okin to argue that these accomplished women have been so misled as to choose an oppressive lifestyle. There is something condescending, even patriarchal, about such a claim. The women themselves see in their new life important values. For example, they see in the mikvah ceremonies "women-centered spiritual celebration of women's bodies, cycles, sexuality, and procreative power."[16] They also see an important opportunity for bonding with one another.

By persisting in advocating secular feminist arguments that are intolerant of important religious values, secular feminists run the risk of turning patriarchal. At its most abstract level, I define patriarchy as a hierarchical system in which control flows from the top. Thus, in a patriarchal system, men oppress other men and not only women. This is why ending such a system is better for all of humanity and not only women. Furthermore, the top of the pyramid in a patriarchal system could be filled with either men or women (witness Margaret Thatcher) without its patriarchal nature being changed. If Western feminists are now vying for control of the lives of immigrant women by justifying coercive state action, then these women have not learned the lessons of history, be it colonialism, imperialism, or even fascism. After all, such feminists "think that the best community is one in which all but their preferred . . . [gender] practices are outlawed." Ironically, that is the definition Okin quotes for fundamentalists.[17]

Okin occupies a difficult position. She is right to be concerned about her sisters, and not to look the other way in the face of their oppression. She even shows some recognition of the fact that her views may be too severe. For this reason, she briefly refers at the end of her piece to "negotiations about group rights."[18] It is unclear, however, whether these negotiations are recommended with all minority groups or limited to those that satisfy the "requirement of internal liberalism."[19]

The issue is actually of some urgency to me personally. As a Muslim who believes that many oppressive practices attributed to Islam are either cultural ones or ones that resulted from a patriarchal interpretation of religious text, what should I do about oppressive behavior among some Muslims in this country? Two types of behavior come to mind. The first involves such actions as violence against women; the second involves such behavior as wearing a head scarf.

In the first instance, the perpetrator of violence against a woman (or man) is guilty of assault and battery under Islamic law, and his punishment is as severe as his crime.[20] Furthermore, as a good Muslim, I may not shift my responsibility for correcting the situation to the legal system and turn my face the other way.[21] If the system fails to take appropriate protective action, I have a duty to step in and try to end the violence by any legitimate means available to me.[22] The Qur'an enjoins me to take personal responsibility to correct the situation myself, the best way I possibly can.[23] The moral values underlying this analysis are clearly shared universally, by people of faith as well as secularists. There is no dilemma here, nor a viable cultural or religious excuse that could justify violence against women.

The other example is more complicated. Why is it oppressive to wear a head scarf but liberating to wear a miniskirt? The crux of the explanation lies in the assumptions each side makes about the women involved and their ability to make choices. But suppose, for the sake of argument, that I too find covering one's head oppressive, and that it is not required religiously. Should I now organize to force those sisters to bare their heads? Should I organize to ensure that they do not pass their values to their children?

Clearly, I could build a limited united front with secular feminists and try to foster popular sentiment against self-oppressive choices. But my Islamic training and knowledge of my community tell me that many of these Muslim sisters have thought seriously about the issue of covering their heads and have reached conclusions different from mine. Forcing them to abandon their religious choices is not only patronizing but fundamentally un-Islamic! Islam has an established etiquette of difference, by which I may explain my position to other Muslims without ever claiming exclusive access to the truth or becoming coercive.[24]

Only God knows the truth, and what Okin and I believe in today as the truth may be quite different from what we may believe to be the truth ten years hence. After all, I was a Marxist in the seventies. Nevertheless, that part of the women's movement I belonged to in the United States (the Society for Women in Philosophy) made every effort to make room within it for women of faith, on the basis of feminist nonhierarchical principles. Today, as a Muslim, I am prevented by my religion, through the dual concepts of *shura* and freedom of *ijtihad*, from imposing my views on other Muslims, let alone non-Muslims. In that I am guided by the example of Imam Malik, who repeatedly rejected the Caliph's offer to adopt his jurisprudence as the official jurisprudence of the state.[25] In characteristic modesty, he was unwilling to deny others their freedom of *ijtihad*. After all, only God knows best.

Siding with the Underdogs

YAEL TAMIR

*

IN HER excellent essay, Susan Okin draws attention to inherent tensions between group rights and women's rights. She points to the fact that establishing group rights which enable minority cultures to preserve themselves may not be in the best interest of the girls and women of these cultures. This is patently true.

This brief comment supports Okin's claims and argues that the importance of the issues she raises extends far beyond feminist concerns. It is a word of caution, calling upon liberal political theorists and liberal political activists to acknowledge that group rights strengthen dominant subgroups within each culture and privilege conservative interpretations of culture over reformative and innovative ones. Women rarely belong to the more powerful groups in society, and protectors of women's rights do not affiliate themselves with conservative segments. It follows, then, that women, and those who strive to protect their rights and equal status, are among the first to be harmed by group rights. Their plight, however, is not unique. It is shared by all those who wish to diverge from accepted social norms and question the traditional role of social institutions.[1]

Why do group rights serve best the interests of those members of society who are powerful and conservative? To begin with, the notion of group rights as it is often used in the current debate presupposes that "the group" is a unified agent. Rights are bestowed upon "the group" in order to preserve "its" tradition and defend "its" interests. Identifying "the" tradition and "the" interests of "the" group becomes a precondition for realizing these rights. Consequently, internal schisms and disagreements are perceived as a threat to the ability of the group to protect its rights. Group leaders are therefore motivated to foster unanimity, or at least an appearance of unanimity, even at the cost of internal oppression.

Attempts to achieve unanimity are particularly dangerous in those communities which lack formal, democratic decision-making processes. Under such circumstances it is the elderly of the tribe, members of councils of sages, who determine the groups' norms and interests. Members of such bodies are commonly men, who endorse a rather orthodox point of view. Social norms and institutions place these individuals in a dominant position, and group rights consolidate this position even further. Granting nondemocratic communities group rights thus amounts to siding with the privileged and the powerful against those who are powerless, oppressed, and marginalized, with the traditionalists (often even the reactionary) against the nonconformists, the reformers, and the dissenters.

The conservative nature of group rights is reinforced by the justifications adduced in their defense. The group is granted rights in order to preserve its culture, language, tradition. These are described, by most defenders of group rights, in nostalgic, nonrealistic terms. They are depicted as authentic, unique, even natural. Those who attempt to consolidate the conservative way of doing things are therefore portrayed as loyal defenders of the group; those who strive for social transformation and cultural reformers are perceived as agents of assimilation who betray the group and its tradition. The former are depicted as virtuous individuals who dedicate themselves to the common good; the latter are suspected of being motivated by narrow self-interest—of giving priority to short-term preferences for personal comfort and prosperity over long-term commitments to the welfare of the community.

Agents of social and cultural change are portrayed as feebleminded individuals who are tempted by the material affluence of the surrounding society, as those who sell their soul to an external devil in exchange for some glittering beads. It therefore seems legitimate to criticize, scorn, even persecute them. This is the fate of Reform Jews who are often portrayed by the Orthodox establishment as irresponsible, weak-minded, pleasure-seeking individuals who wish to escape the burden of Judaism in order to adopt a less demanding lifestyle. Reform Jews, Orthodox argue, are swayed by the external (and superficial) beauty of Christian architecture and ceremonies. The reforms they offer are seen as grounded in mimicry, as an attempt to be like the Gentiles rather than as a call to reevaluate Judaism and offer ways in which it can answer the needs and challenges of modernity. Reform Judaism is therefore portrayed as a threat to the *survival* of Judaism rather than as an attempt to save it.

The use of the term *survival* in the context of the debate over group rights is common, yet alarming. It misdescribes what is at stake, intensifying the cost of change and fostering the belief that any violation of social and religious norms, any reform of traditional institutions and the group's customary ways of life, endangers its existence and must therefore be rejected.

Moreover, it intentionally obscures the distinction between two kinds of communal destruction: the first results from external pressures "exhorted" by nonmembers; the second, from the desire of members of the community. It is clear why we ought to protect a community and its members in cases of the first kind, but should we protect a community also against the preferences of its own members? Is it just, or desirable, to allow those who aspire to preserve the communal tradition—often members of the dominant and privileged elite—to force others who have grown indifferent or even hostile to this tradition to adhere to that tradition?

Obviously, defenders of group rights who use the term *survival* to denote cultural continuity tend to give priority to this end over and above individual rights. Charles Taylor's discussion of the Canadian case demonstrates this order of priorities: "It is axiomatic for the Quebec government that the *survival* and flourishing of French culture in Quebec is a good. . . . It is not just a matter of having the French language available for those who might *choose* it. . . . Policies aimed at *survival* actively seek to *create* members of the community, for instance, in their assuring that future generations continue to identify as French speakers."[2]

It should be clear by now that in the Canadian case, as well as in the debate between Orthodox and Reform Judaism, the term *survival* refers not to the actual survival of the community or its members but to the survival of the traditional way of life. It is used to justify the taking of extreme measures, including disregard for individual rights and forceful suspension of internal criticism, for the sake of preventing change. But is there a reason to prevent a particular way of life from undergoing change? Should one protect a community against cultural revisions or reforms, even radical ones, if these are accepted by its members? The answer to the above question depends on the motivations one may have for protecting cultures or traditions.

An approach that is grounded in the right of individuals to pursue their lives the way they see fit must support individuals who wish to reform their tradition and change their lifestyle as much as it ought to support individuals who wish to retain their traditional way of life. It must be attentive to the kind of life plans individuals adopt and pursue, without prejudging in favor of conservative options. It should therefore defend individuals against pressures to conform and protect their choice to reform their tradition or even exit the community altogether. The opposite is true for an approach that is motivated by the desire to defend endangered cultures. Such an approach must favor conservative forces over reformist ones, even at the price of harming some individual interests. Obviously multiculturalism that is grounded in the former approach is friendly to feminism, while that which is grounded in the latter is not.

It is not uncommon for liberal scholars to offer theoretical justifications for the first kind of approach while supporting policies that accord with the second. In *Liberalism, Community, and Culture*, Kymlicka justifies group rights by making references to the wellbeing of individuals. And yet he sides with those who aspire to defend traditional ways of life from both external and internal pressures. This becomes clear in his discussion of mixed marriages. When Indians who live on reservations marry outsiders, a problem of overcrowding emerges that does not permit the allocation of land to each family. Kymlicka describes two traditional solutions to this problem: the first adopts *the blood criterion* according to which "only those with a certain proportion of Indian blood can be full members of the band, so non-Indians spouses never acquire membership, nor do children if they have less than the required proportion."[3] The second endorses a criterion based on *kinship*, according to which every member of the family has the same status, but Indian women who enter into mixed marriage lose their status.[4] Both solutions disadvantage those members who deviate from the norm of marrying within the tribe, and the kinship approach specifically discriminates against women.

Is there a nondiscriminatory solution to the problem of overcrowding? Such a solution will have to surrender the (reactionary) assumption that in order to retain their identity, all members of the tribe must adopt traditional kinds of occupations which are land-consuming. Why not encourage some Indians to acquire new types of occupations? Why is it assumed that the only way Indians can retain their identity and tradition is by adhering to the same kinds of occupations their forefathers, or foremothers, pursued? Why is it that Americans from Philadelphia can retain their American identity despite the fact that they live cultural, social, and professional lives very different from those of their agrarian predecessors, while Indian men and women can retain their identity only if they preserve a way of life that is as similar as possible to the one experienced by previous generations?

A great deal of paternalism is embedded in the assumption that while "we" can survive change and innovation and endure the tensions created by modernity, "they" cannot; that "we" can repeatedly reinvent ourselves, our culture, our tradition, while "they" must adhere to known cultural patterns. These assumptions are particularly damaging for women who can improve their social status only by challenging traditional norms. If a society cannot undergo change while retaining its identity, then the aspiration of women to improve their social position necessarily comes into conflict with the rights of the group.

If, however, culture and tradition are seen in a less static light, then reformers could be seen as contributing to the preservation of the communal identity no less than conservatives. The fate of a culture, a language, or a religion ought to be determined by its members. For that purpose one must grant cultural, religious, national rights to individuals rather than to the community as a whole. The difference between granting cultural or religious rights to individuals and granting them to groups is evident if one compares the status of the Reform movement in Israel and in the United States. In the

United States religious rights are individual rights—under these condition the Reform movement flourishes, as a large percentage of American Jews choose to affiliate with it. In Israel, on the other hand, religious rights are granted to each religious community. The search for a unified voice that represents the Jewish community provokes a struggle among the different Jewish movements. The Orthodox, who succeeded in presenting themselves as the sole authoritative representatives of Judaism, attempt to disqualify all other versions, especially the Reform one. The Reform movement is thus presented as a threat to the continued existence of the Jewish people, and its members are deprived of their religious rights. Unlike Orthodox institutions, Reform ones receive almost no financial support from the state; the teachings of the Reform movement are not part of Jewish studies in schools; and Reform rabbis cannot perform marriage. Consequently the Reform movement finds it very hard to form an Israeli branch. As a result, in Israel (unlike the United States), individual Jews are unable to make a free choice concerning the way they would like to practice their religion.

This analysis can teach three lessons: first, we should have a realistic, less sentimental view of traditional communities and a less static view of culture. We ought to recognize that cultures are permanently changing and developing, and that there is no reason to "freeze" a culture in order to preserve it. Cultures hostile to change are less likely to flourish and stand the risk of degeneration. Second, we should trust the ability of individuals to withstand change and reform their traditions and lifestyle without surrendering completely their particular identity. Third, we must entrust the faith of the community to its individual members. We ought then to empower individuals by granting them individual rights. In so doing, we may protect the rights of the less powerful and less conservative members of each group to live their lives and preserve their identity the way they see fit. In so doing, we may also provide help and support for agents of cultural and social change in general, and in particular for defenders of women's rights.

"Barbaric" Rituals?

SANDER L. GILMAN

*

Susan Okin's essay reminds us of the importance of a historical sensibility in our reflections on religious ritual and cultural tradition. Her language and images take us back 150 years to a time when the focus would not have been on female circumcision / ritual mutilation but on infant male ritual circumcision / ritual mutilation. (Yes, that term was used!) Those terrible Jews: their repulsive practice of marking the bodies of their male children was, as Enlightenment "thinkers" such as Voltaire stated, clear proof of their inherent inhumanity. A European *liberal*—the Italian physician Paolo Mantegazza, the widely read sexologist of the late nineteenth century and the physician who introduced cocaine into Europe—could write: "Circumcision is a shame and an infamy; and I, who am not in the least anti-Semitic, who indeed have much esteem for the Israelites, I who demand of no living soul a profession of religious faith, insisting only upon the brotherhood of soap and water and of honesty, I shout and shall continue to shout at the Hebrews, until my last breath: Cease mutilating yourselves: cease imprinting upon your flesh an odious brand to distinguish you from other men; until you do this, you cannot pretend to be our equal. As it is, you, of your own accord, with the branding iron, from the first days of your lives, proceed to proclaim yourselves a race apart, one that cannot, and does not care to, mix with ours."[1] Is this not, with small linguistic shifts concerning gender, the tone and stance of Susan Okin?

For Okin the culprit is the "patriarchy," but a patriarchy that still evokes the image of Jewish difference. No less a feminist critic than Susannah Heschel has shown in her insightful work on the image of the Jews in contemporary feminist thought[2] how the "patriarchy" comes to be defined as the special domain of the Jews. Okin's covert history of the "patriarchy" begins with the binding of Isaac as the key to all further images of the exclusion of women. (It is this text, one might add, that has been used over and over again since the Enlightenment as proof of the Jewish proclivity to murder their own as well as others' children. If you are willing to kill your own child, a bit of sexual mutilation is nothing in comparison! The story of Isaac remains the basis for accusations of ritual murder even today in contemporary Russia.) In the Enlightenment, Jews could become good citizens, but they could do so only if they were no longer different—only if they abandoned their ritual practices, such as the *brith melah*, the circumcision of the male child. Such practices are passé, they constitute an invasion of the autonomy of the individual, they cause infection, even death, and, at the bottom, they are signs of barbarism that must be overcome if one wants to be "modern." Today, women are "free" only when they relinquish all ritual practices that "set them apart," and, says Susan Okin, I will tell you what they are!

Such a desire underlies Okin's argument—all people can become happy and well adjusted once they *abandon* those pesky rituals of difference that I don't like. And she makes her distinction between the normal and the repressive based on her notion of what is acceptable practice—i.e., the absence of certain types of ritual—which (surprise, surprise) turns out to mirror her own beliefs and background. She labels certain practices as "barbaric" because these rituals create (in the mind of the external observer) physical images of difference. In doing so, she speaks for those engaged in ritual practices, for they are clearly victims of false consciousness and are unable to speak for themselves. No one could really want to undertake such rituals or have them done to their offspring, and therefore it is clear that women who might advocate them are "brainwashed." And in this state they require someone else to speak for them. Thus in the Enlightenment the friends of the Jews, such as Christian Wilhelm Dohm and the Abbé Grégoire, spoke *for* as well as supporting the civic emancipation of the Jews—certainly advocating their civil rights but also underlining their need to become "healthy" members of a civil society if they were to become "real" citizens!

Okin claims that "women" are the prime victims of religious practices. But can one really speak of "women" as a unitary category? Her representation of "woman" as a singular, monolithic category is difficult to understand at the close of the millennium. The claims of the Enlightenment construction of "man" as a universal category have been (at least since Theodor Adorno's critique of the Enlightenment) shown to be specious; Okin's "woman" suffering under the patriarchal rule of "religion" is a similar composite creature. And "she" must be rescued from the ignorance of superstition by "Western" women! But women are unquestionably a diverse group, as feminists have argued for over a decade. The very claim that Western (or Westernized), bourgeois (and, yes, white) women can speak for all women was exploded in discussions within and beyond the United Nations meeting on the status of women held at Nairobi more than a decade ago.

Recently claims of speaking for the Other have surfaced in the debates about ritual circumcision. The discussion by American "women of color," such as Alice Walker, about the bodies of women in Africa in the context of rituals of infibulation has been dismissed by many women within these cultures as misrepresenting their own autonomy. Critics such as my colleague Martha Nussbaum, Yael Tamir, and Frances Kamm expressed their opposition to this practice because of its impact on female sexual pleasure. Pleasure was and is the "rub." The antisemite Ezra Pound once remarked to his friend Charles Olson: "There was a Jew, in London, Obermeyer, a doctor . . . of the endocrines, and I used to ask him what is the effect of circumcision. That's the question that gets them sore . . . that sends them right up the pole. Try it, don't take my word, try it. . . . It must do something, after all these years and years, where the most sensitive nerves in the body are, rubbing them off, over and over again."[3] Sexual pleasure is defined as the sexual pleasure of the speaker; sexual pleasure is defined as that which reflects the "sensitivity" of the self as opposed to the Other. Sensitivity (of body and of spirit) is measured by the absolute notion of a physical body reacting uniformly to "simple" stimuli. Is it not clear that even sexual pleasure is as much a reflex of the mind as of the body! The centuries-long debates about the physical and the spiritual nature of the sexual experience are now resolved in such a context—only the body speaks, and that independent of the psyche! It is not possible to have sexual pleasure with a "mutilated" body, says the Western view of all ritual alterations of the genitalia.

Tropes about the psychopathology of those who circumcise and are circumcised appear from St. Paul to the present. In the seventeenth century, when decircumcision came into vogue, Gabriel Groddeck commented that the Jews "imagined their fleshly desires could be fulfilled by greater stimulation if they were provided with that little bit of skin, and they believed also that they would give pleasure to their harlots and sweethearts, who broadcast in a depraved manner their very great pleasure if they have slept with a man who either never had the foreskin removed or had it restored."[4] In our own time, in the *Journal of the American Medical Association*, my colleague Edward O. Laumann released a study of circumcision based on a sample of 1,410 men eighteen to fifty-nine years old, interviewed in 1992 as part of his National Health and Social Life survey.[5] He argued (based on that most modern of devices, the self-reporting questionnaire) that circumcised men, because of the loss of sexual pleasure, are forced to resort to weirder and weirder sexual practices (such as fellatio—yuk!) in order to get pleasure. (But pleasure they do receive, according to even this account.) Here he seems to be following the claims of John R. Taylor at the University of Manitoba, whom he does not cite. Taylor claims that the small sheath of foreskin tissue removed during circumcision is filled with extremely sensitive nerve endings and mucus membrane cells and its removal permanently blunts erotic stimulation.[6] Laumann's reading of sexual experimentation on the part of circumcised men—given his claim of an increase in sexually transmitted diseases of all kinds among such men—is a pathological one. And this is the model followed in the debates about female genital mutilation. Only intact genitalia can give pleasure. But is it possible that the projection of Western, bourgeois notions of pleasure onto other people's bodies is not the best basis for anybody's judgment?

Observers of the new Africa know that discussion of the "ritual mutilation" of the African body has been a hallmark of the modernizing forces, whether the body was that of a man or of a woman. Indeed, the wide practice of adult *male* circumcision has been actively opposed by the African National Congress in the new South Africa as a sign of the barbarism of ancient tribal rituals—much to the dismay of the ritually circumcised Xhosa president of the new South Africa, Nelson Mandela. Mandela understands and advocates the ritual of circumcision because it formed his (and his contemporaries') experience of themselves as Xhosa men. What many in South Africa understand is that abolition of ritual will not further the stated goal of the creation of a complex, composite South Africa identity. The problem with ritual circumcision is the risk of infection, not the creation of "difference"; the answer should be found in the introduction of antisepsis, as was the case with infant male circumcision in the nineteenth century. Jews, for the most part, did not abandon infant male circumcision, but they certainly altered the form of its practice. Not abolition but medicalization would seem to be the reasonable remedy for the morbidity and mortality resulting from all such practices. The question of pleasure should be left to the culture that defines it.

It would seem that the acculturation of infant male circumcision through its medicalization in the late nineteenth century could be paralleled by the claim (heard recently in Egypt) for the medicalization of female circumcision and its limitation to a symbolic cutting of the labia minora. Indeed, as noted in Egyptian sources, one of the problems with the label of "female genital mutilation" is that it refers to a very wide range of practices. But such a movement for reform rather than abolition would take seriously the claims of ritual in the culture in which it was practiced. Such rituals are not "merely" superstition, even if they are debated hotly as such within the religious cultures themselves. For one person's defining ritual is another person's meaningless superstition. Remember that Helene Deutsch, one of the mothers of psychoanalysis, foresaw a future when the pains of childbirth would be so lessened that women would seek new rituals of investiture and coming-of-age and would turn to infibulation as their new ritual practice.[7]

Here is the problem with Okin's worldview. In advocating the abolition of other people's rituals, she fails to see ceremonial acts in her own culture as limiting and abhorrent. Only the world of ritual *as she defines it* holds this power. The "bizarre" rituals of Anglo-American culture are for her the norm. The power invested in Anglo-American class structures is less evident to her than the power invested in the patriarchy in those ritualized belief systems that she rejects.

Promises We Should All Keep in Common Cause

ABDULLAHI AN-NA'IM

*

T HEORIZING of the kind reflected in Susan Okin's essay (or Samuel Huntington's *Clash of Civilizations*) sometimes influences public policy and thereby affects the lives of individuals and communities. Moreover, such influence often extends beyond, and sometimes contradicts, a theorist's own intentions. Beginning from these premises, I wish to raise two sets of questions about Okin's argument and outlook.

First, can liberal theorists deliver on the promises they make to members of cultural minorities within what Okin calls "Western liberal cultures"? Do such theorists in North America and Western Europe have a clear understanding of the *meaning* of cultural membership in a minority culture in Western societies, as a daily existential experience and not merely a theoretical construct? And are they willing and able to act in solidarity with minority groups in advancing the objectives those communities now hope to achieve through assertions of group rights? In particular, if they encourage young women to repudiate the integrity and cohesion of their own minority culture, how can the theorists then help to sustain the identity and human dignity of those women?

Second, are liberal theorists concerned about the wider implications of their thinking even for their own official agenda—let alone other equally important issues—at home or elsewhere in the world? For example, will the solution Okin is proposing for Western countries be resented as hegemonic imposition, whether among minorities in the West or in non-Western societies, thereby becoming counterproductive for gender equality in practice? What are the likely consequences of her approach on the dynamic of the human rights movement at large?

In raising these issues, my frame of reference is the system of international human rights standards, rather than the cultural norms of the majority, as reflected in its conceptual and legal order, social and political institutions, and public discourse. I rely on human rights as a shared frame of reference because the alternative would be cultural hegemony at home and imperialism abroad. Most generally, then, my question is: What are the implications of an exclusive focus on gender issues for other human rights standards throughout the world?

I AGREE with Okin's view that nearly all cultures discriminate against women—especially many of the minority cultures on whose behalf claims of group rights are being made in Western societies. I also share her commitment to the elimination of all forms of discrimination against women and girls everywhere as a human rights imperative. The main difference between our positions pertains to the possibility of *comprehensive* strategies for the protection of all human rights throughout the world. What I emphasize is that, in seeking to eliminate discrimination on grounds of sex, one should avoid encouraging discrimination on grounds of race, religion, language, or national origin.

For example, Okin's analysis makes no reference to economic and social rights (such as the right to an adequate standard of living and education) although these concerns constitute much of the rationale of group rights. This omission is particularly significant because failure to accept these as *human rights* is a clear indication of liberal "cultural relativism" in the wider debate about the universality of human rights.

Moreover, while citing examples of discrimination against women and girls from various parts of the world, Okin does not seem to be concerned with the resolution of those problems in non-Western societies. I am therefore wondering whether her proposed solution for the elimination of gender discrimination within minority cultures in the West is detrimental to the achievement of this objective itself globally, let alone to the realization of a more comprehensive view of human rights everywhere.

Okin says that she prefers that a minority culture be "encouraged to alter itself so as to reinforce the equality of women—at least to the degree to which this value is upheld in the majority culture," rather than "become extinct (so that its members would become integrated into the less sexist surrounding culture)." The sense of ultimatum is of course clear even in her preferred solution. Minority cultures are told: either change to achieve gender equality in the private lives of your families and communal affairs, or perish. But Okin does not offer any comment on the implications of cultural extinction for members of minority cultures. Moreover, it is interesting to note that Okin is willing to accept the degree of gender equality upheld by the majority culture. Whereas the minority culture faces an ultimatum in meeting the standard set by the majority culture, the latter can take its own time in achieving gender equality at the level set by international human rights norms, if ever.

I am not suggesting, of course, that either minority or majority should be allowed to practice gender discrimination, or violate some other human right, because they believe their culture mandates it. In particular, I emphasize that all women's rights advocates must continue to scrutinize and criticize gender discrimination anywhere in the world, and not only in Western societies. But this objective must be pursued in ways that foster the protection of all human rights, and with sensitivity and respect for the identity and dignity of all human beings everywhere.

In other words, I say that all cultures must be held to the same standards not only of gender equality but also of all other human rights. While gender equality is a serious problem in some minority cultures in the United States, for example, racism and economic and social rights are large problems for the majority culture. So American human rights advocates should be equally concerned with all human rights issues that are problematic in their own situation, though some of them may have one particular focus or another for practical reasons. Only by engaging in such an "internal discourse" can American human rights advocates gain the moral credibility required to encourage such discourse elsewhere. This in turn will generate "cross-cultural dialogue" to promote consensus on truly universal human rights norms and their principled and sustainable implementation throughout the world.[1]

I am also suggesting that compliance with human rights standards cannot be achieved in a principled and sustainable manner except through the internal dynamics of the culture concerned. For that to happen, the argument for gender equality has to be made within the frame of reference of minority culture, and for economic rights within the framework of liberal Western cultures. The persistence of gross structural, as well as social, racism in the United States should clearly indicate the difficulty of achieving the type and degree of cultural transformation necessary for the effective implementation of a universally accepted human rights norm. It would also be both salutary and instructive for liberal intellectuals to try to "encourage their own culture to alter itself" in order to accept and implement economic and social rights as human rights.

I SUGGESTED earlier that human rights must be the commonly agreed frame of reference for debate. Some people are tempted to say that economic and social "claims," such as health care or housing, are not "really" human rights. But how would they respond in the face of a similar denial of human rights standing for gender equality? Whatever grounds exist for human rights standing for the one apply to the other. This does not leave the issue to arbitrary assertions and claims. Rather, the task is to provide specific criteria and a process for balancing different values. So, what are human rights, and how are they established or ascertained?

Intuitively, human rights are claims we make for the protection of our vital interests in bodily integrity, material well-being, and human dignity. To secure respect for our rights, we must concede the right of others to make similar claims for the protection of their vital interests. Practically speaking, the normative content of human rights has been established by international treaties negotiated and adopted by governments within the framework of the United Nations and regional intergovernmental organizations.

Both intuitively and practically, group rights are human rights, at least under the rubric of the right of "peoples" (not states or nations) to self-determination, as provided for in the first article of both the International Covenant on Economics, Social and Cultural Rights and the International Covenant on Civil and Political Rights.[2] To be sure, self-determination is commonly understood to refer to political independence for formerly colonized people. But now that that objective has been achieved, attention must be given to "internal" self-determination as the ultimate goal and rationale of political independence everywhere.

According to the first article of the two covenants, self-determination means that a people "freely determine their political status and freely pursue their economic, social and cultural development"; and "freely dispose of their natural wealth and resources. . . ." For a people (which can mean a cultural minority) to exercise these rights, the members must be able to act *collectively as a community*, rather than simply as individual "citizens" of a country. At the same time, since the two covenants and other instruments also (actually primarily) protect individual rights, it is not a question of choice between individual and group rights. Rather, it is a matter of mediation of conflicts between individual and group rights, as well as within each set of rights.

As Okin has clearly shown in the case of gender equality, group and individual rights can conflict. There are also the usual questions about agency and representation when claims are being made on behalf of corporate entities. But this simply means that the concept and precise content of group rights need to be clarified and mediated in relation to other rights and concerns. After all, there are conflicts between different individual rights, as can be seen in debates about the scope of freedom of expression in relation to "hate speech." Long-standing civil rights, even within such a highly developed domestic constitutional order as that of the United States, are constantly renegotiated among competing constituencies, as can be seen in the case of abortion or affirmative action. Yet no one would suggest abolishing the underlying rights because of problems with their scope and implementation.

In conclusion, I would also note that "uniculturalism" has its own problems, for women and men, girls and boys, as individuals and communities. So, unless we can actually deliver on the promises we made when raising skeptical doubts about multiculturalism, we should work to maximize its benefits and reduce, if not eliminate, its disadvantages. Instead of repudiating multiculturalism because it risks persistent gender inequality, let us work within minority cultures for the internal transformations outlined earlier.

Between Norms and Choices

ROBERT POST

*

SUSAN OKIN'S primary claim, that there is a deep tension between feminism and multiculturalism, seems unambiguously correct. While multiculturalism celebrates the diversity of cultures, including necessarily the diversity of gender roles that preoccupy these cultures, the enterprise of feminism is dedicated precisely to constraining the available repertory of such roles. By inviting us carefully to focus on this tension, Okin's article usefully exposes ambiguities in our concepts of both feminism and liberal multiculturalism.

Okin defines feminism as the "belief that women should not be disadvantaged by their sex, that they should be recognized as having human dignity equal to that of men, and that they should have the opportunity to live as fulfilling and as freely chosen lives as men can." This definition is certainly attractive, for such values as "dignity" and "freedom" seem incontrovertibly desirable. Yet Okin's confrontation with multiculturalism puts this definition under considerable pressure. Take, for example, the culture of Orthodox Ashkenazi Judaism, which possesses strongly distinct and patriarchal gender roles. The culture disqualifies women from important religious rituals, and it assigns them primary responsibility for the care of the home and children.

If we assume that these distinct gender roles do not violate any legal rules prohibiting sexual discrimination, and that these roles are (perhaps counterfactually) entirely confined to what Okin calls "the private sphere," we may ask whether Okin would nevertheless object to endowing this culture with what Will Kymlicka calls "external protections." External protections, while not using the force of the state to impose minority cultural norms upon individuals, empower a culture to "protect its distinct existence and identity by limiting the impact of the decisions of the larger society."[1] Such protections might, for example, authorize the Orthodox Jewish community to educate its children in Yiddish or to take distinctive religious holidays.

Okin strongly implies that she would not support according the culture of Orthodox Ashkenazi Judaism external protections, because it would be "in the best interests of the girls and women" if such a culture were "to become extinct," so that girls and women could integrate themselves "into the less sexist surrounding culture." Okin's repeated references to "older women" who are "co-opted into reinforcing gender inequality" suggest that Okin would persist in this position even if (as seems likely) Orthodox Jewish women were to report that they did not view themselves as "disadvantaged," because they had "freely chosen" their lives, which they found "fulfilling," and because they viewed themselves as having equal "dignity" with men, although that dignity was expressed through distinct social roles.

This suggests that the feminist enterprise paradoxically encounters unsettling difficulties when faced with an alien culture that fully and successfully normalizes patriarchy. In the effort to sustain the feminist indictment of such a culture, a typical response is to create the possibility of indicting "co-opted women" with false consciousness by translating evaluative ethical concepts like "dignity" and "freedom" into seemingly more objective and external criteria. Thus in the body of her paper Okin summons what appear to be more descriptive standards, like "disparities in power between the sexes."

But the more that the feminist project is pushed in this direction, the more it loses its status as a general set of constraints on permissible gender roles and becomes a full-blown articulation of a particular vision of gender roles defined by measurable standards of equality. Not only would such an articulation naturally resist the competing visions of gender roles exemplified by multiculturalism, but it would also be more controversial and difficult to defend within our own culture. The feminist challenge to liberal multiculturalism thus forces feminism to sharpen its own normative claims.

The tension identified by Okin also underscores fundamental ambiguities in the position of liberal multiculturalism, at least as that position is defended by proponents like Will Kymlicka. As a multiculturalist, Kymlicka argues that the capacity of individuals "to make meaningful choices depends" in significant measure on their access to their own "cultural structure,"[2] and that liberalism, which prizes "freedom of choice" and "personal autonomy,"[3] thus has good reason to support the preservation of cultural structures. But, as a liberal, Kymlicka also concedes that some cultures are intrinsically hostile to personal autonomy and freedom of choice, and he therefore argues that (in theory at least) minority rights should not be construed so as to "enable a group to oppress its own members."[4]

Within the perspective of liberal multiculturalism, therefore, culture both sustains and constrains individual freedom. This means that we may ask about any given cultural norm whether its enforcement should be interpreted as a precondition of choice, or instead as a restraint on choice. Okin's essay illustrates how Kymlicka systematically evades this question. He collapses it into the issue of whether minority groups ought to be accorded the right to enforce "internal restrictions," which he defines as curtailments of "the basic civil and political liberties of group members."[5] Kymlicka opposes in theory awarding minority groups such rights.

Okin's emphasis on the "private sphere," however, reminds us that cultures can be deeply oppressive in ways that neither involve minority rights nor formally violate political and civil liberties. Cultures can be oppressive because of the values or social roles they inculcate. They can, as Okin points out, repress the value of autonomy and significantly impair "our capacity to question our social roles." Much of Okin's argument, in fact, depends upon her piercing the organic unity that Kymlicka seems often to assume exists between a culture and its members. Okin thus speaks of "roles that cultural groups *impose* on their members" (my emphasis). It seems difficult to defend external protections for such impositions on the liberal grounds advanced by Kymlicka.

But when, exactly, do the pervasive influences of a culture become "impositions"? The problem is particularly difficult because the distinction cannot be evaluated merely by reference to contemporary notions of political and civil liberties. This is because such liberties are themselves the result of a long and complex historical evolution within the context of our own Western culture. We have little or no idea what civil rights would be necessary to protect individual autonomy within the context of an alien structure of culture. It may be, for example, that liberalism would espouse very different forms of civil and political liberties if attempting to check the "imposition" of gender roles in the circumstances of a pervasively patriarchal culture like Orthodox Ashkenazi Judaism.

Okin's essay reminds us, therefore, that distinguishing between enabling and oppressive cultural norms is a fundamental challenge of liberal multiculturalism, a challenge that has yet to be successfully confronted.

A Varied Moral World

BHIKHU PAREKH

*

MANY A classical liberal argued that since the liberal view of life was grounded in the fundamental truths of human nature and represented more or less the last word in human wisdom, nonliberal communities at home and abroad should be persuaded and, if necessary, pressured and coerced to assimilate into it. This belief informed J. S. Mill's attitudes to the native peoples, the Basques, the Bretons, the Scots, and the Francophones in Quebec, and formed the basis of his justification of British colonialism in India and elsewhere. Alexis de Tocqueville shared his view. And since the fun-loving people of Tahiti lacked moral seriousness and high ideals and were little different from "sheep and cattle," Kant wondered "why they should exist at all" and what the universe would lose if they disappeared altogether.

Most liberals today are more tolerant of nonliberal communities—some for prudential reasons, others on the basis of suitably reinterpreted liberal principles—and believe that they should be allowed the right to preserve their cultures. Contemporary liberals are, however, troubled by the fact that the communities concerned sometimes engage in practices that violate important liberal values. While acknowledging the obligation to respect minority cultures, liberals rightly think that toleration cannot be unconditional. Where, then, should they draw the line?

The standard liberal strategy is to derive the limits of toleration from the grounds of it. For Will Kymlicka, who has given more thought to this subject than most liberals, minority cultures should be tolerated because a stable culture is the necessary precondition of human flourishing. This means that no cultural practice should be tolerated that denies its members a measure of autonomy, choice between worthwhile options, dissent, and the right of exit, all of which he takes to be constitutive of human well-being. Since he defends cultural autonomy on liberal functionalist grounds, it is hardly surprising that he arrives at the liberal functionalist criteria of toleration.

Susan Okin shares Kymlicka's approach and pushes it further. For her, minority cultures should enjoy the right to autonomy only when and only to the extent that they respect what she calls the "fundamentals of liberalism." She singles out the equality of the sexes as one of these fundamental values and takes it to imply that women should enjoy not only equal dignity and rights but also the opportunity to lead equally fulfilling lives and to question their socially prescribed roles.

In her view many minority cultures are deeply sexist, treating women as inferior and relying on a combination of ideological and legal coercion to condition them into accepting their subordinate status, with the result that they often lead miserable lives and grow up without a sense of self-respect and capacity for autonomy. Okin insists that respect for other cultures should not become a shield for sexism, that their self-proclaimed leaders, mostly male and conservative, should not be allowed to become their sole spokesmen, and that since multiculturalism implies respect for cultural autonomy, feminists should not give it their uncritical support.

I find most of the substantive conclusions of her excellent and passionately argued paper unexceptionable. She is right to argue that respect for cultures can never be unconditional and condone acts of inhumanity and oppression. This is why respect for human beings does not necessarily entail respect for their cultures, for the latter might show no respect for human beings. Clitoridectomy and other most horrendous forms of female genital mutilation, forced or child marriages, callous treatment of rape victims, and suppression of women in general are all unacceptable practices and should be disallowed. In recent years Britain has produced even more horrifying cases. Since the communities concerned are unable to set their cultural house in order, even the staunchest champions of cultural autonomy have reluctantly asked the law to intervene.

While agreeing with Okin's conclusions on these and related matters, I feel uneasy about her reasons and her wider theoretical framework. First, since she concentrates on extreme cases, she ignores
the problems involved in judging other cultures. Clitoridectomy on
children is unacceptable because it causes irreparable harm to help-
less victims on the basis of dubious and contested beliefs. In some
communities, however, it is freely undergone by adult, sane, and
educated women after the birth of their last child as a way of regulating their sexuality, or reminding themselves that they are from now
onward primarily mothers rather than wives, or as a religious sacrifice of what they greatly value for the sake of their children and
family, or as a symbolic break with one phase of life. I wonder
whether Okin wishes to ban this and why. Again, polygamy is unacceptable if limited to men, but what if women were also given the
right to marry multiple partners? It then does not offend against the
principle of the equality of the sexes. Indeed, it does not seem to
violate any of the central liberal values, for it is based on uncoerced
choice by adults, respects individual differences of temperament and
emotional needs, encourages experiments in living, relates to the
realm of privacy with which the liberal state is expected not to interfere, and so on. I am not sure that Okin's theoretical framework is
rich enough to deal with these questions satisfactorily.

Second, when Okin disallows such practices as clitoridectomy and
forced marriages, she does so on the ground that they violate the
fundamentals of liberalism. Liberalism refers to the way a set of values are defined, related, and integrated into a more or less coherent
doctrine. Since the values can be defined, related, and integrated in
several different ways, there are many kinds of liberalism, none true
or claiming the allegiance of all liberals. Liberalism therefore has no
fundamentals, though, of course, different liberals may confer such
a status on different values. Okin is free to regard certain values as
fundamental but wrong to claim the authority of the entire liberal
tradition for them.

Even if we accepted certain values as fundamental liberal values,
they are surely not self-evident and beyond criticism. Okin needs
to show why they are worth accepting, especially in relation to non-
liberals who deny their validity. It would not do to say that these

are values which "they" must accept, both because we are not all agreed about them and because nonliberal citizens are now part of us. To insist that they must abide by our fundamentals is to expose ourselves to the same charge of fundamentalism that we make against them, and to rely solely on our superior coercive power to get our way.

Okin's approach also faces another danger. If minority cultures are to be required to conform to fundamental liberal values, there is no reason to stop with the equality of the sexes. One could equally consistently require them to respect such other fundamental liberal values as autonomy, individualism, choice, free speech, and open internal debate. This amounts to saying that minority cultures should be respected only if they become liberal, an extreme form of intolerance that shows scant respect for their identity. There is a fine line to be drawn between respecting others' cultural differences and requiring them to conform to certain minimal values. Okin's appeal to the "fundamentals of liberalism" to set the limits of tolerance does not allow her to draw it.

Third, although Okin rightly insists on the equality of the sexes, her definition of it is too broad to be practicable or even acceptable. It is one thing to say that women should enjoy equal dignity and rights, but an altogether different thing to say that they should also be equally autonomous, free to challenge their social roles, unconstrained by the subtle controls of patriarchal cultures, and so forth. The latter criteria are too complex to measure and apply across cultures, and rest on a view of equality that is unlikely to command universal consensus. Furthermore, in some societies women are treated as inferior when young or unmarried but are revered and enjoy superiority over men when they reach a certain age, become grandmothers, lead virtuous lives, or display unusual qualities. This is why these societies present the apparent paradox of being both sexist and accepting, even welcoming, of women leaders in all walks of life. Since women at different stages of life or in different relationships are perceived differently and endowed with different rights, the "woman" is too oversimplified an abstraction to allow us to appreciate the diversity of her status, roles, and power in the diverse array of human cultures. We need more nuanced and complex notions of equality than Okin proposes.

There is also the further question of how women themselves perceive their situation. If some of them do not share the feminist view, it would be wrong to say that they are victims of a culturally generated false consciousness and in need of liberation by well-meaning outsiders. That is patronizing, even impertinent, and denies them the very equality we wish to extend to them. This is not to say that they might not be brainwashed, for sometimes they are, but rather that we should avoid the mistaken conclusion that those who do not share our beliefs about their well-being are all misguided victims of indoctrination. In Britain several well-educated white liberal women have in recent years converted to Islam, or returned to some aspects of traditional Judaism, because, among other things, they found these traditions' views of intergender relations more convincing or emotionally more satisfying than conventional alternatives. There is a lesson here for both liberals and feminists.

In France and the Netherlands several Muslim girls freely opted for the *hijab*, partly to reassure their conservative parents that they will not be corrupted by the liberal culture of the school and partly to reshape the latter by indicating to both white and Muslim boys that they were not available for certain kinds of activities. The *hijab* was in their case a highly complex autonomous act intended both to remain within the tradition and to challenge it, to accept the cultural inequality and to create a space for equality. To see it merely as a symbol of their subordination, as many French feminists did, is to miss the subtle dialectic of cultural contestation.

Fourth and finally, Okin fails to appreciate the full force of the challenge of multiculturalism and the opportunity it offers to liberals to deepen and enrich their self-understanding. Like Will Kymlicka she takes liberalism as self-evidently true, asks how it can accommodate minority cultures, and more or less reduces multiculturalism to a discussion about group rights, which is but a small and minor part of it. What is clumsily called multiculturalism is a revolt against liberal hegemony and self-righteousness. For centuries liberal writers have claimed that theirs was a transcultural and universally valid moral and political doctrine representing the only true or rational way of organizing human life. A multiculturalism that rejects this extraordinary claim is not so much a doctrine as a perspective. Pared down to its barest essentials and purged of the polemical exaggeration of its defenders and detractors, it represents the view that culture provides the necessary and inescapable context of human life, that all moral and political doctrines tend to reflect and universalize their cultural origins, that all cultures are partial and benefit from the insights of others, and that truly universal values can be arrived at only by means of an uncoerced and equal intercultural dialogue.

From a multicultural perspective the liberal view of life is culturally specific and neither self-evident nor the only rational or true way to organize human life; some of its values, when suitably redefined, may be shown to have universal relevance, but others may not; and liberal relations with nonliberal cultures should be based not on dogmatically asserted liberal values but on a critical and open-minded dialogue.

Multiculturalism deflates the absolutist pretensions of liberalism and requires it to acknowledge its contingent historical and cultural roots. Since no culture exhausts the full range of human possibilities, multiculturalism also requires liberalism to become self-critical and to engage in an open-minded dialogue with other doctrines and cultures. It rejects the liberal claim to enjoy the monopoly of moral good and to be the final arbiter of all moral values, its crude and tendentious division of all ways of life and thought into liberal and nonliberal, and its persistent tendency to avoid a dialogue with other cultures by viewing them as nothing more than minority cultures whom it would "grant" such rights as it unilaterally determines.

In her moving paper Susan Okin offers a liberal theory of multiculturalism in which liberalism is the hegemonic interlocutor and sets the parameters for nonliberal cultures. We need instead a multicultural theory of liberalism that both cherishes and appreciates the limitations of the great liberal values, assigns them their proper but limited place in the moral world, and provides a framework of thought and action in which different cultures can cooperatively explore their differences and create a rich and lively community based on their respective insights. When allowed to flourish under the minimally necessary moral constraints, multiculturalism is likely to generate radically novel ways of conceptualizing and structuring intergender relations that cannot but deepen and broaden the hitherto somewhat parochial feminist sensibility. Far from being the enemy of women, it gives them the unique historical opportunity to pluralize and transform radically the universally hegemonic and boringly homogeneous patriarchal culture that damages both women and men alike.

Culture beyond Gender

SASKIA SASSEN

*

THE FRAMING of an argument matters. Susan Okin's argument hinges on the fact that group rights tend to be cultural rights, and that the norm in most cultures is an inequality between men and women that works to the overwhelming disadvantage of women. This framing makes her argument persuasive and well-supported by an enormous body of evidence. Thus organized, the debate between feminists and supporters of group rights is resolutely won by the feminists, and I would place myself squarely in the latter field.

Even if we consider group rights as a way of protecting the importance of "culture" for one's sense of self and for richness of experience/norms/rituals, I agree with Okin that the price for women and girls of ensuring this "richness" through an oppressive culture is too high, and indeed many women in such cultures have in some way said so.

Consider the case of immigrant women in the United States. The individual rights that the culture grants to women can help immigrant women become empowered and develop stronger senses of self. A large literature shows the impact of immigrant women's regular wage work and improved access to various public realms on their gender relations.[1] Women gain greater personal autonomy and independence while men lose ground. Women gain more control over budgeting and other domestic decisions, and greater leverage in requesting help from men in domestic chores. Also, their access to public services and other public resources gives them a chance to become incorporated into the mainstream society—they are often the ones in the household who mediate in this process. (It is likely that some women benefit more than others from these circumstances; we need more research to establish the impact of class, education, and income on these gendered outcomes.) Group rights did not help these immigrant women achieve a greater sense of self and confidence.

But even a small shift in the frame of Okin's argument leads to important questions. What if "culture" cannot be made to pivot so exclusively on the oppression of women? Having worked with a number of disadvantaged, poor immigrant groups in the United States, mostly originating in the types of cultures (for example, Latino culture) that Okin centers on, I find that the oppression of the men and boys is in some cases so severe (on their jobs, in school) that the minority culture serves as an instrument for their engaging with or escaping from the dominant culture. This can engender forms of solidarity between men and women that aid survival in a hostile or discriminating host culture. Similarly with the presumption of moral superiority as mothers I have seen deployed by some middle-class women in the United States and Germany vis-à-vis poorer immigrant women: here, too, the site of pain and anger shifts away from intracultural gender inequalities to intercultural dynamics of domination/discrimination. We know that for many immigrants in Europe, both men and women, *not* becoming citizens is a way to protest racism. We have seen similar choices in the United States before the new 1996 immigration law. (This law has resulted in an explosion of naturalizations because the new law discriminates against those with immigrant status; under these conditions, becoming a citizen emerges as a defense of last resort to protect some basic entitlements.) Under conditions of such intercultural tension and discrimination, cultural affirmation is not simply a way to preserve intracultural gender inequality, and the analysis of culture cannot be centered analytically exclusively on the organization of gender, even if the latter is enormously important.

To be sure, in most cultures women are at an enormous disadvantage. So I am not disputing Okin's major conclusion about group rights. But if we overlook the joint presence of (and relations between) a dominant (or "host") and minority culture, we may be overlooking the many sources of pain and rage produced by intercultural engagements. Engaging, whether by necessity or by choice, with a dominant culture may lead in turn to the "need" (in both men and women) for the refuge of one's culture also in areas other than gender. Further, the pain and rage produced by this engagement with the dominant culture may change key aspects of gender organization in the minority culture. The case of Latino immigrant women in the United States indicated earlier is an instance.

In raising these issues, I have not addressed the question of group rights per se. I agree with Okin that group rights are a problematic (and mostly) unnecessary vehicle for achieving greater gender equality—or, if you will, a less gendered society. Instead I want to emphasize the risk of centering culture exclusively on the organization of gender, especially when (as in the contemporary United States and Europe) both the men and the women of many minority cultures may feel oppressed by a dominant/host culture. Recognizing the importance of dynamics other than those of gender in a context of discrimination/persecution against one's group may well be strategic for eliminating or reducing the conditions that led to the demand for group rights in the first place. Rather than rejecting group rights as such, the analytic and political focus may well have to negotiate intracultural gender inequalities at the center of Okin's concerns and intercultural oppression that frequently lies at the origins of the experienced need for group rights.

In the global cities where I have done much of my research and fieldwork, intercultural battles and alliances are a marking condition for men and women and children.[2] Isolating their culture of origin as an equally marking and exclusive condition becomes almost impossible. Women and children emerge often as the carriers or the agents of this new, hybrid condition of negotiation. This negotiation may turn out to be crucial in the fight against the norms that legitimate the oppression of women (and children) in many of the minority cultures described by Okin.

Liberalism's Sacred Cow

HOMI K. BHABHA

*

LIBERALS have a way of occupying the high moral ground while keeping the lower depths finely covered, moving convincingly from "causes" to cases, balancing theory and practice. What are the possibilities of maneuver in the midst of such fluency? I welcome Susan Okin's central argument that "there is considerable likelihood of tension . . . between feminism and a multiculturalist commitment to group rights for minority cultures," which persists even when the latter are claimed on "liberal grounds." This is a useful corrective to the prevailing orthodoxy that establishes "equivalences" between disadvantaged groups, aggregating "communities of interest" without doing the hard work of specifying rights and interests, shying away from conflicts within, and between, minorities.

Let me, however, tweak the sacred cow by the tail (rather than indulging in the phallic fandango of taking the bull by the horns) and suggest that the force of Okin's feminist advocacy rests on a restricted understanding of the "liberal grounds" on which feminism and multiculturalism might negotiate their differences about rights and representations. Okin's view of the interface between feminism and multiculturalism is so focused on the "conflict" generated by the antifeminist and patriarchal effects of criminal cultural defense that, against her own best advice, she allows herself to produce "monolithic," though gender-differentiated, characterizations of minority, migrant cultures—kidnap and rape by Hmong men, wife-murder by immigrants from Asia and the Middle Eastern countries, mother-child suicide among Japanese and Chinese provoked by the shame of the husband's infidelity.

The cultural defense plea is the ethnographic evidence that, for Okin, invokes the basic idea that the defendant's cultural group regards women as subordinates whose primary purpose is to serve men sexually and domestically. By contrast, "Western liberal cultures" (a phrase Okin uses to identify which side she is on) may discriminate between the sexes in practice, but the protection of domestic law produces an enabling and equitable familial culture for girls and women. Writing as I am from London, I can most readily address the British experience. The British civil liberty group Liberty would demur at Okin's description of the egalitarian and empowering "Western" domestic scene. *Human Rights and Wrongs*, an alternative report to the UN Human Rights Committee, concludes that one-third of all reported crimes against women in Britain result from domestic violence and take place at home; in London, in 1993, one woman in ten had been assaulted by her partner. Adult women and children are overwhelmingly more likely to become the victims of violence at home than on the street or at the workplace.

But I am, here, less concerned with the domestic perspective than with the more global cultural assumptions that animate Okin's arguments. Her narrative begins by pitting multiculturalism against feminism but then grows seamlessly into a comparative and evaluative judgment on minority cultures (largely represented by cultural defense cases) delivered from the point of view of Western liberal cultures (represented by the eloquent testimony of academic feminists). In my view, however, issues related to group rights or cultural defense must be placed in the context of the ongoing lives of minorities in the metropolitan cultures of the West if we are to understand the deprivation and discrimination that shape their affective lives, often alienated from the comforts of citizenship. Minorities are too frequently imaged as the abject "subjects" of their cultures of origin huddled in the gazebo of group rights, preserving the orthodoxy of their distinctive cultures in the midst of the great storm of Western progress. When this becomes the dominant opinion within the liberal public sphere—strangely similar to the views held by patriarchal elders within minority communities whose authority depends upon just such traditionalist essentialisms and pieties—then minorities are regarded as virtual citizens, never quite "here and now," relegated to a distanced sense of belonging elsewhere, to a "there and then."

Entreating us to pay attention to the less formalized institutions and spheres of social life, to regard the "internal differences and . . . the private arena" within which the unequal relations of gender become visible, Okin surprisingly chooses to characterize gender roles within immigrant communities largely on the basis of information submitted as evidence for criminal cultural defense procedures. By relying so heavily on the context and discourse of the courtroom, where cultural information is being mobilized for very specific ends (to answer a criminal charge, to argue for the mitigation of a sentence), Okin is in danger of producing the monolithic discourse of the cultural stereotype. Cultural stereotypes may well have the ring of truth and accurately register aspects of a cultural tradition. However, they are reductive insofar as they claim, for a cultural "type," an invariant or universal representability. Stereotypes disavow the complex, often contradictory contexts and codes—social or discursive—within which the signs and symbols of a culture develop their meanings and values as part of an ongoing, transformative process.

However rhetorically effective, or politically expedient, it may be to found an argument on "citations" gleaned from cultural defense cases, they cannot provide Okin with an understanding of "patriarchy" as it is played out in culturally diverse societies or experienced within migrant communities in racially biased Western liberal cultures. Put "patriarchy" in the dock by all means, but put it in a relevant context; sentence sexism but specify it too. "Patriarchy" in India, for instance, intersects with poverty, caste, illiteracy; patriarchy in liberal America is shored up, among other things, by racism, the gun culture, desultory welfare provision; patriarchy and gender-relations in migrant communities are complicated by the fact that women, young and old, are often caught between the benevolent patronage of a Western liberal patriarchy and the aggressivity of an indigenous patriarchal culture—threatened by the majority culture and challenged by its own "second" generation. Okin's ahistorical view of "patriarchy" ("most of the peoples of Africa, the Middle East, Latin America, and Asia . . . are quite distinctly patriarchal") and her monolithic, deterministic notion of Culture itself ("[Muslim] Law allows for the whipping or imprisonment . . . and culture condones the killing or pressuring . . .") combine to form a dangerous presumption that many of the world's other cultures— cultures that are not "Western majority cultures"—exist in a time warp. They are represented as having no local traditions of protest, no indigenous feminist movements, no sources of cultural and political contestation. For an argument that rightly suggests that we should take our moral and political bearings from the "internal differences" that mediate power relations within communities, Okin's casts a gaze on "non-Western" peoples that comes resolutely from above and elsewhere. Her version of liberal feminism shares something of the patronizing and stereotyping attitudes of the patriarchal perspective.

Indeed, her monolithic distinction between the West (liberal) and the Rest seems to consign the South to a kind of premodern customary society devoid of the complex problems of late modernity. The opposite is often the case. It is the fragile political and economic fate of postcolonial societies, caught in the uneven and unequal forces of globalization, to suffer in a heightened and exaggerated form the contradictions and ambiguities that inhabit the Western world. Take, for instance, the proposals for new divorce laws in China.[1] Formulated to make divorce difficult, to punish male adultery, and to protect wives who are increasingly cast aside for mistresses known as "little honeys," the proposed laws have met a mixed, contested response within the feminist community. China is certainly not my idea of a liberal society, but this has not prevented a debate within the Chinese women's movement that has taken up a number of "liberal" positions and pitted them against other radical and emancipatory alternatives. As the *Times* reports, "Women's advocates have been bitterly split by the proposals, with some calling them needed protections for women while many younger feminists and sociologists call them a regressive move in a country where the Communists have a history of paternalistic meddling. . . ." "We need to make a distinction between law and morality," as an expert on sex issues at the Chinese Academy of Social Sciences said. Whether married women should seek "progressive" state protection or aggressively reject the surveillance of such a pastoral (patriarchal) state is an argument that has many resonances with such discussions

in the "West." We can make common cause with such a controversy—on one side or the other—but not without undertaking the
work of cultural translation that would enable us to specify the concept of "paternalistic meddling" in relation, say, to the American
liberal understanding of patriarchical influence, when discussing
policy issues concerned with family law, the role of women, and the
regulatory norms of the State.

I do not wish to press the tired and overused charge of "Euro-
centrism" against such an argument. What is considerably more
problematic than the inappropriate application of "external" norms
is the way in which the norms of Western liberalism become at once
the measure and mentor of minority cultures—Western liberalism,
warts and all, as a salvage operation, if not salvation itself. With a
zealousness not unlike the colonial civilizing mission, the "liberal"
agenda is articulated without a shadow of self-doubt, except perhaps an acknowledgment of its contingent failings in the practice of
everyday life. If the failures of liberalism are always "practical,"
then what kind of perfectibility does the principle claim for itself?
Such a campaigning stance obscures indigenous traditions of reform
and resistance, ignores "local" leavenings of liberty, flies in the face
of feminist campaigns within nationalist and anticolonial struggles,
leaves out well-established debates by minority intellectuals and activists concerned with the difficult "translation" of gender and sexual politics in the world of migration and resettlement.

Okin's concluding suggestion that "non-co-opted" younger
women should be represented in negotiations about group rights (so
that they may be protected from the more collusive, co-opted older
women) smacks just a little of "divide and rule." It may be useful to
recognize that for many postcolonial peoples, who now count as the
"minorities" of Western multiculturalism, liberalism is not such a
"foreign" value nor quite so simply a generational value. Asian and
Middle Eastern feminists, for instance, from the 1920s onward,
have been deeply engaged in those contradictions of the liberal tradition that become particularly visible in the colonial and postcolonial
contexts, and carry over into the contemporary lives of diasporic or
migratory communities. Such an agonistic liberalism, with a colonial and postcolonial genealogy, has to struggle against "indige-

nous" patriarchies—political and religious—while strategically negotiating its own autonomy in relation to the paternalistic liberalisms of colonial modernity or Westernization. An agonistic liberalism questions the "foundationalist" claims of the metropolitan, "Western" liberal tradition with as much persistence as it interrogates and resists the fundamentalisms and ascriptions of indigenous orthodoxy. An awareness of the ambivalent and "unsatisfied" histories of the liberal persuasion allows "us"—postcolonial critics, multiculturalists, or feminists—to join in the unfinished work of creating a more viable, intracultural community of rights.

Should Sex Equality Law Apply to Religious Institutions?

CASS R. SUNSTEIN

*

I AM IN general agreement with Susan Moller Okin's excellent essay. In particular I agree with her suggestion that sex equality often conflicts with a respect for minority cultures. Frequently such cultures do not permit girls and women to live as freely as boys and men, and the consequence is that general approval of "multiculturalism" can collide with the goal of achieving equal life prospects for men and women.

In these brief remarks I seek to draw out some more concrete implications from this general claim. My principal concern does involve feminism and multiculturalism, but it is somewhat narrower than Okin's—not minority cultures in general, but religious institutions in particular. As Okin shows, religious institutions are sometimes a source of discriminatory practices, and hence respect for the autonomy of religious institutions may undermine the goal of sex equality. Conflicts between sex equality and religious institutions create severe tensions in a liberal social order.[1] They raise the obvious question: What is the appropriate domain of secular law insofar as government seeks to control discriminatory behavior by or within religious institutions?[2]

In addressing this question, I focus on an insufficiently explored puzzle. In the United States (and in many other nations), it is generally agreed that most ordinary law, both civil and criminal, is legitimately applied to religious organizations. Thus, for example, a secular government may prohibit members of a religious institution from engaging in murder, kidnapping, or assault, even if those acts are part of religious ceremony and guided by religious precepts. At the same time, it is generally agreed that there are important limits on the extent to which the law of sex discrimination is legitimately applied to religious organizations. The state does not, for example, require the Catholic Church to ordain women as priests, and religious institutions are plainly permitted to engage in acts that would be unacceptable discrimination if carried out by a secular entity.[3] Interference with religious autonomy is usually prohibited if sex discrimination is the ground for the interference.

An important commonplace of liberal theory and practice might therefore be deemed the *asymmetry thesis*. According to the asymmetry thesis, it is unproblematic to apply ordinary civil and criminal law to religious institutions, but problematic to apply the law forbidding sex discrimination to those institutions. Thus it is uncontroversially acceptable to prevent priests from beating up women (or anyone else) as part of a religious ceremony, or to ban Orthodox Jews, even if they are sincerely motivated by the religiously founded idea of a male rabbinate, from assaulting Reform women rabbis; but it is often thought unacceptable to ban sex segregation in education,[4] or to prohibit religious groups from excluding women from certain domains.

What is the source of this asymmetry? The answer bears on some of Okin's more abstract arguments (as well as abstract arguments made by others), and it may also help in specifying their content. If, for example, the asymmetry thesis holds, there are grounds to qualify or perhaps even to reject Okin's argument; if the thesis does not hold, it may be legitimate or even mandatory to implement a sex equality principle in some controversial ways, by interfering with widespread religious practices.

I

Consider the following potential conflicts between sex equality and freedom of religion, conflicts that arise in one or another form in many nations:

1. Certain Jewish synagogues educate boys separately from girls, and certain Jewish schools refuse to admit girls. Some Jewish girls and their parents contend that this is a form of sex discrimination that contributes to sex-role stereotyping.

2. A Catholic university refuses to tenure several women teachers in its canon law department. A disappointed faculty member complains that this is a form of employment discrimination.[5] The university responds that courts cannot intervene in a religious matter of this kind.

3. A young man trains and studies for ordination to the priesthood of the Society of Jesus. He is repeatedly subjected to sexual harassment by two ordained priests. The harassment takes the form of unwanted sexual comments, propositions, and pornographic mailings. He brings suit for employment discrimination.[6]

4. Mormon employers engage in various practices of sex discrimination in employment. They refuse to hire women for certain jobs; they claim that being male is a bona fide occupational qualification for certain positions. These practices are undertaken in the private sector, in institutions that both have and do not have explicitly religious functions.

5. A Western nation allows immigrant men to bring in multiple wives. It recognizes their polygamous marriages and various discriminatory practices (including "assigning" teenage girls to older men for marriage) that accompany certain religious convictions.[7]

Freedom of religion has a central place in the liberal tradition, and in the United States, as elsewhere, the law forbidding sex discrimination contains important exemptions for religious institutions. The law itself permits bona fide occupational qualifications based on sex, and courts have said that the free exercise clause of the Constitution requires courts to refrain from adjudicating sex discrimination suits by ministers against the church or religious institution employing them—even though ministers could certainly complain of assault or rape.[8] This principle has been read quite broadly, to apply to lay employees of institutions (including high schools and universities) whose primary duties consist of spreading the faith or supervising religious rituals.[9]

As I have suggested, the resulting doctrine is a puzzle in light of the fact that almost no one believes that in general, such organizations can be exempted from most of the law forbidding civil and criminal wrongs. The puzzle is not only obvious but also important, for there is good reason to believe, as Okin shows, that some of the most pernicious forms of sex discrimination are a result of the practices of religious institutions, which can produce internalized norms of subordination.[10] The remedy of "exit"—the right of women to leave a religious order—is crucial, but it will not be sufficient when girls have been taught in such a way as to be unable to scrutinize the practices with which they have grown up. People's "preferences"—itself an ambiguous term[11]—need not be respected when they are adaptive to unjust background conditions; in such circumstances it is not even clear whether the relevant preferences are authentically "theirs."

There is a further problem. Seemingly isolated decisions of individual women to subordinate themselves may help establish and reproduce norms of inequality that are injurious to other women. Women interested in sex equality therefore face a collective action problem; rational acts by individual women can help sustain discriminatory norms. To say the least, it is not obvious how a liberal society should respond to this problem. But some measures prohibiting sex discrimination may make things a bit better.

II

To answer the underlying question, to understand the asymmetry principle, and to obtain something of a legal perspective on Okin's claims, we have to step back a bit and say a few more general words about the relationship between liberal law and religious institutions. In the United States, there is a sharp and continuing debate about whether a state may apply "facially neutral" laws to religious institutions. A law is facially neutral if it does not specifically aim at religious practices or belief; thus a law banning the burning of animals or the use of peyote is facially neutral, whereas a law banning the Lord's Prayer is facially discriminatory.

Under current law in the United States, any facially neutral law is presumed to be constitutionally acceptable.[12] The validity of all facially neutral laws may be deemed "the *Smith* principle," after the highly controversial Supreme Court decision that established it.

The *Smith* principle seems to be undergirded by two distinct ideas. The first involves an understanding of *the relationship between liberty and democracy*: A secular law that is neutral on its face does not interfere with religious liberty, properly conceived. On this view, the democratic process is a sufficient safeguard against laws that are facially neutral but oppressive; the very neutrality (and hence generality) of such laws guarantees against oppressiveness, for when a number of groups are subject to law, they are likely to mobilize against them and to prevent their enactment (unless there are very good reasons for them).

The second basis for the *Smith* principle is one of *administrability*: Even if some facially neutral laws raise serious questions in principle, it is very hard to administer a test for constitutionality (or political legitimacy) that would require a kind of balancing of the opposing interests. The best defense of the *Smith* principle is that even if it protects religious liberty too little, it comes close to protecting religious liberty enough—and it does so with the only principle that real-world institutions can apply fairly and easily. The best challenge to current law is that many facially neutral laws do impose substantial burdens on religion; that they lack sufficient liberal justification; and that institutions, including judicial institutions, are perfectly capable of drawing the appropriate lines.

III

Let us now turn to the reasons why a state might be permitted to apply the ordinary civil and criminal law to religious institutions, but be proscribed from applying the law of sex discrimination to such institutions.

1. The first possibility is that a state may interfere with religious practices only when it has an especially strong reason for doing so (sometimes described as a "compelling interest"). The ordinary criminal and civil law provides that reason; the law that forbids sex discrimination does not. On this view, it is one thing for a state to prohibit murder or assault. It is quite another thing for a state to forbid discriminatory practices.

There can be no doubt that an intuition of this kind helps explain current practice; indeed, I believe that it plays a large role in establishing the conventional wisdom and the asymmetry thesis itself. And the idea would have some force if the ordinary criminal and civil law always directed itself against extremely serious harms. But it does not. The ordinary law prohibits torts that are often relatively modest (intentional infliction of emotional distress, little libels, minor assaults even without physical contact). And the state is not forbidden to apply the tort law when the underlying torts are modest. Under the *Smith* principle—and before that case there was little doubt about the basic idea as applied to ordinary tort law—there is no weighing of the state's interest to assess its magnitude. Thus, for example, state law that bars the intentional infliction of emotional distress is entirely applicable to religious institutions; like everyone else, priests and rabbis are not permitted to tell people that their children have just been run over by trucks, even if those people are religious enemies.

Religious organizations are thus subject to relatively trivial civil and criminal law. Nor is it easy to explain why the interest in being free from sex discrimination is, in principle, so modest as to be weaker than the interests that underlie various aspects of the ordinary civil and criminal law. Often the interest in eliminating sex discrimination appears to be far stronger than the particular interest involved in ordinary law.

Now perhaps it will be responded that the *Smith* principle is wrong, and that religious institutions should not be subject to ordinary civil and criminal law when the state lacks an especially strong reason for invoking its ordinary law. This idea lay behind the Religious Freedom Restoration Act, invalidated by the Supreme Court in 1997 as beyond Congress's power, but exemplifying a widely shared view about the nature of religious liberty. We have seen the direction in which an argument to this effect might go, and I will return to the question shortly. The important point for present purposes is that a rejection of the *Smith* principle does not entail approval of the asymmetry between the law banning sex discrimination and ordinary law. If the *Smith* principle is wrong, some ordinary law cannot legitimately be applied to religious institutions; whether the law of sex discrimination can be so applied depends on the nature of the relevant "balancing," an issue to which I now turn.

2. It might be thought that a prohibition on sex discrimination would impose a substantial burden on religious beliefs and practices, or even strike at their heart, whereas the ordinary civil and criminal law does not. On this view, the *Smith* principle is wrong; some exemptions are necessary.[13] But the reason for any religious exemptions is respect for religious autonomy, respect that can coexist with ordinary civil and criminal law, but not with the law forbidding sex discrimination. For some religious institutions, a secular mandate of (a controversial conception of) sex equality would be intolerable, whereas application of ordinary law fits comfortably, in general, with their beliefs and practices. The asymmetry thesis might be defended on this ground.

The argument is not entirely without force. Sometimes ordinary civil or criminal law is fully consistent with the norms of religious institutions; indeed, such law often grows directly or indirectly out of religious norms. And it is also possible to imagine requirements of sex equality that would go toward the heart of religious convictions. But in its broadest form, the argument is quite fragile. Some aspects of ordinary civil and criminal law do strike against practices and beliefs that are central to some religions. Consider, for example, the law forbidding animal sacrifice or the use of drugs, or even laws forbidding certain kinds of assault and imprisonment. And some aspects of the law of sex discrimination interfere not at all with some religious beliefs and practices.

Now it is possible that as a class, ordinary civil laws coexist easily with most religious practices and beliefs, whereas the law of sex discrimination does not. But to the extent that this is so, it is a contingent, time-bound, highly empirical fact, one that bears little on the question of principle from the liberal point of view. If, for example, it were thought that the state could interfere with religious practices only when the interference was not serious, we could not justify a sharp asymmetry between ordinary law and the law of sex discrimination. We would have to proceed in a more fine-grained way; we would not endorse the asymmetry thesis.

3. It might be possible to defend the asymmetry thesis with the suggestion that an appropriate test depends on both the strength and nature of the state's interest and on the extent of the adverse effect on religion. A weak interest (in preventing, let us suppose, merely technical libels) might be insufficient to justify any intrusion at all; an illegitimate interest (in, say, preventing the strengthening of a religion hostile to the political status quo) would be ruled entirely off-limits; an "overriding" interest (in, for example, preventing murder) would justify any intrusion, no matter how severe; a strong or "compelling" interest would justify most intrusions. Most cases would therefore be easy. The hardest problems would arise where a strong or "compelling" interest were matched by a plausible claim that the interference would seriously jeopardize the continuing functioning of the relevant religion.

In principle, a standard of this sort seems the best one for a liberal social order to adopt, though to adopt it, we would have to have a high degree of confidence in those who would administer it. Such a standard would require courts (or other institutions) to decide which aspects of the civil and criminal law were sufficiently justified. Thus we could imagine reasonable judgments in favor of a legal ban on killing and torturing animals, but against a legal ban on peyote, on the ground that the former created a risk to third parties. The legitimacy of applying principles against sex discrimination to religious institutions would depend on an assessment of the strength of the interest in those principles and the extent of the interference with religious institutions.

Doubtless different outcomes would be imaginable in different contexts, and I do not mean to sort out all of the conceivable dilemmas. My basic point is that the asymmetry between most civil and criminal law and the law banning sex discrimination could not be sustained. Under the standard I am proposing, some ordinary law would not legitimately be applied to religious institutions, and some of the law banning sex discrimination could be so applied. The legal standard would force a candid assessment of the nature of the intrusion and the strength of the underlying interest, and not rest content with homilies (by no means followed with most civil and criminal law) about the legitimate autonomy of religious institutions.

IV

I offer three simple conclusions:

1. There is a plausible rationale for the view that a liberal social order should accept all laws that do not discriminate "on their face" against religious institutions and practices. This principle would authorize the application to those institutions of most civil and criminal law and also of law forbidding sex discrimination. Though plausible, this principle is not in the end acceptable, because it would allow the state to subject religious institutions to laws that substantially burden those institutions, or even strike at their heart, without at the same time serving a sufficiently important governmental purpose.

2. It is not only plausible but also correct to say that a liberal social order should disallow facially neutral laws if they (a) interfere in a significant way with religious practices, or impose a substantial burden on religious institutions, and (b) are not supported by a legitimate and sufficiently strong justification. But this idea does not support a categorical distinction between ordinary civil and criminal law and laws forbidding sex discrimination. In many cases, the idea would allow religious institutions to immunize themselves from ordinary law, but forbid them to immunize themselves from the law prohibiting discrimination on the basis of sex.

3. There is no plausible rationale for the view, embodied in the practice of many liberal cultures, that it is unproblematic to apply ordinary civil and criminal law to religious institutions, but that it is problematic to apply, to those institutions, laws forbidding sex discrimination.

This conclusion means that there is no *general* barrier to applying such laws to religious institutions. Whether it is legitimate to do so depends on the extent of the interference with religious convictions and the strength of the state's justification. Reasonable people can reach different conclusions about particular cases; but it would follow that in at least some of the cases traced in section I above, the religious practice would have to yield.

I conclude that the implicit conflict between the asymmetry thesis and Okin's essay poses no problem for Okin, and that one specification of her argument shows why the asymmetry thesis cannot be sustained.

How Perfect Should One Be?
And Whose Culture Is?

JOSEPH RAZ

*

I FIND MYSELF in broad agreement with Susan Okin's concerns, and, so far as practical politics goes, probably little separates us. However, I share neither some of the views that Okin attacks, nor some of those she accepts. In a sense I am a stranger to this debate,[1] but the seriousness of the issues raised by Okin made me agree to write a brief rejoinder to her thoughtful article.

Okin focuses her criticism on "defenders of multiculturalism [who] confine their defense of group rights largely to groups that are internally liberal." I plead not guilty to any charge of advocating the protection of distinct cultures, if their existence is taken to be an unconditional good in itself, or a good conditional only on the desire of their members to see those cultures preserved. Furthermore, while I believe that in certain circumstances groups have rights, I do not believe that those rights play a particularly important role in the argument for multiculturalism, or in the implementation of multicultural policies. On these points, I am at one with Okin. She is not interested in defenses of multiculturalism that depend on the good of cultural diversity as such, or on the sheer desire of people to see their own culture preserved. She seems sympathetic to multiculturalism to the extent that it contributes to the quality of people's life. And she is critical not of multicultural group rights but of any protection of cultural diversity that perpetuates their oppressive practices. See, for example, the doubts she raises regarding some uses of the cultural defense in criminal trials: "the primary concern," she writes, "is that, by failing to protect women and sometimes children of minority cultures from ... violence, cultural defenses violate women's and children's rights to equal protection of the laws." But the defenses she objects to protect individual, not group, rights. Contrary to her declared intention Okin's concerns have little to do with group rights. They focus, quite rightly, on the harm some cultures inflict on their members, or—more precisely—the harm they inflict on women.

I think that Okin underestimates the problem with multiculturalism. It suffers from all the difficulties she mentions, but from others equally serious. Many, perhaps most, of the cultures represented in the West have a long tradition of intolerance toward (some) nonmembers. Many, perhaps most, are intolerant of many of their own members. Repression of homosexuality is probably as widespread as discrimination against women. Intolerance of dissent within the community is widespread, as is blindness to the needs of many people whose physical abilities or disabilities, or psychological needs, fail to conform to the approved ways of the community.

If what I will call for brevity's sake "multicultural measures" are to be taken only with regard to cultural groups that embrace and pursue the right degree of toleration and freedom toward both their own members and others, then none will qualify. On this, Okin is absolutely right. But we will not qualify either. Who "we" are is a moot point. But if "we" includes all those who are not candidates for the benefits of special multicultural measures, then we are homophobic and racist, indifferent to the poor and disadvantaged at least as much, though not necessarily in the same ways, as all those cultural groups for the sake of whose members multicultural measures are adopted. It is probably true that in the recent past we, or some of us, have improved the situation of women in society. But not only are we a long way from eradicating injustice to women; we are even further away from eradicating other injustices in our societies. I expect Okin agrees to all this. She is merely concerned to point out that we should fight for justice for women in other cultural groups as hard as we fight for it in society at large. And so we should. But just as we do not cast doubt on the legitimacy of acting for the preservation of "our" culture simply because it is unjust to women, and to many others, so we should not cast doubt on the legitimacy of acting for the preservation of other cultures just because of the injustices perpetrated by them.

It follows that we need to distinguish between general measures in a multiculturalist spirit and measures that perpetrate oppression or violation of basic civil rights. Okin's paper is full of examples of the second kind. Among typical general measures we could mention providing schooling enabling members of cultural communities to learn their own cultures, languages, or religions, supporting cultural institutions, requiring employers to allow employees time off if this is needed for religious or other cultural purposes, and, most important, enhancing an understanding and acceptance of cultural diversity in the population at large, replacing the attitude of a majority that agrees to tolerate minorities with one of coexistence of various groups within the general framework of one civic and political culture. The point of the distinction is that the need to put an end to specific cultural practices, such as parents' marrying off young teenage girls, should not be regarded as a reason to deny respect and general support to the group whose practices they are. We do not reject our culture when we find it replete with oppression and the violation of rights; we try to reform it. We should not assume the right to reject or condemn wholesale the cultures of groups within ours in similar circumstances.

Why is it that, a few people excepted, we think of reforming our culture, rather than of discarding or destroying it? For most of us the thought of discarding or destroying our culture and starting with a clean slate just does not make sense. It is impossible even to envisage what it could mean. Of course, we can imagine, for example, deciding to emigrate to France and trying to shed any trace of our culture, trying to become French through and through. We tend to find such a course of action undignified. We suspect that those who so behave lack self-respect or self-esteem. But we can understand what it is for a person to try to shed one culture and immerse himself in another. We cannot imagine what it is for a whole national community to do the same, let alone start from scratch.

So if we can think of taking steps to put an end to the existence of distinct cultural groups in our midst this is only because we are outsiders to these groups. Members can disown their group and try to assimilate in the majority group—and we should certainly enable them to do so. Or they can strive to change their group. But they cannot responsibly wish for its extinction. Outsiders can, and members can when they see themselves as outsiders. But, particularly horrendous groups excepted, we should not do so precisely because we are outsiders.

These reflections (in conjunction with related considerations) have practical implications: in the first instance, excepting morally repugnant cultures, the state should recognize and support all the cultures significantly represented in it, and encourage respect for them. At the same time, the state should protect all its inhabitants from injustice, whether sexist or some other kind. Just as respect and support for the majority culture does not imply its preservation from change, nor immunity to reform, so with regard to other cultural groups within the country. That this involves difficult problems, with sound values pulling in different directions, is obvious. That no solution to these problems is possible without sacrifice of the promotion of some sound values is equally obvious. The need for sensible multicultural measures arises out of dilemmas generated by imperfect reality. They represent the least worst policy, not a triumphal new discovery.

In all this I feel that I am agreeing with Okin. I'll mention just one central difference. In some ways Okin shows great sensitivity to the significance of social practices. But in others she seems somewhat blind to them, in particular to the fact that the same social arrangements can have differing social meanings, and therefore differing moral significance, in the context of different cultures. This leads her to judge other cultures more harshly than her own, for she is instinctively sensitive to the context of her culture (and mine) and is less likely to misread it.

However, this blindness to the values that other cultures realize, and to the opportunities they afford women and others, has less of an impact on policy decisions than first appears. Practices that are harmless, or even valuable, when pursued within the confines of an independent society, often become oppressive and unacceptable when persisted in by immigrant groups, living as they must within an alien culture. The cultural and moral significance of some of their practices inevitably changes in the new circumstances. And often it changes for the worse: turning what was an ordinary aspect of life into a symbol of alienation, of rejection of one's surroundings, and the like. Once a culture becomes one among several, within a closely integrated political and economic system, practices that used to shape opportunities may come to restrict them. And they may conflict with aspirations legitimately encouraged by the larger society within which members of that community live. It is a mistake to think that multicultural measures can counteract these facts. Nor should they try. They should not aim to preserve the pristine purity of different cultural groups. They should aim to enable them to adjust and change to a new form of existence within a larger community, while preserving their integrity, pride in their identity, and continuity with their past and with others of the same culture in different countries.

Culture Constrains

JANET E. HALLEY

*

Susan Okin correctly observes that women's rights conflicts are extremely salient in debates over "cultural rights." I take this as a sign, however, that women's rights discourse is alive and well, making productive friction on a global scale. What puzzles me is that women's issues are so often thought to exhaust the supply of problems embedded in cultural rights projects.

Culture constrains. Sure, it may liberate too, but efforts to justify cultural rights are characteristically defective to the extent that they insist on the liberation story while suppressing the constraint story. This is, for example, where I would have to disagree with Will Kymlicka, whom Okin addresses as her representative cultural rights spokesperson.

Okin has made an interesting choice, for she shares more fundamental normative commitments with Kymlicka than she does with many advocates of cultural rights. Kymlicka, after all, argues that cultural rights are justified not despite but within liberal theory: when national or ethnic cultures assert power over their members that infringes on individual liberty, he is prepared to be just as critical as Okin. Thus their disagreement appears to be primarily empirical: Do women's rights conflicts have the gravity and frequency that Okin claims they do, or is Kymlicka's relative inattention to them a good register of their marginality and ready resolvability?

I think the problems run much deeper even than that. Consider one argument that Kymlicka makes in his fascinating book *Multicultural Citizenship*.[1] Kymlicka sets up criteria that have the effect of drastically reducing the number of "problem cases" he needs to acknowledge. The underlying conceptual problems suggest that Okin's objections on behalf of women miss more general tensions that are more interesting, more agonizing, and possibly even more productive than the tension between women's freedom and their involvement in culturally structured private spheres.

Kymlicka argues that national and ethnic groups protecting themselves from outsider encroachments do not necessarily thereby threaten the autonomy of insiders. Most often they want only to survive as groups. When that is their goal, he argues, liberal theory cannot object; indeed, it should welcome the provision of meaningful choices to group members. Kymlicka points the finger at religious communities, and away from national and ethnic communities, for seeking to protect their boundaries in ways that constrain members and thus offend liberal tenets; and he is ready to join Okin in objecting, on liberal grounds, when this occurs.[2]

Thus it is an important part of the Okin/Kymlicka empirical dispute that Kymlicka rules out only the *intentional* constriction of members' rights. On his view, if a group-preserving policy has unintended, even if predictable, side effects that infringe individual rights, threats to individual liberties are weak, indirect, and easier to explain away.

The elevation of intention to pivotal status here is problematic. Surely where the liberal model of primordial individual rights is absent or attenuated, it is unlikely that conscious intentions will register the full trade-off between cultural preservation and group-member rights. (The point should be familiar to left-multiculturalist and left-liberal critics, who raise it when the Supreme Court refuses to find racial discrimination without proof of intent. What, the Left quite properly asks, about the strenuous support for white privilege contributed when whites invidiously undervalue and undercompensate people of color *without meaning to?*) More seriously still, Kymlicka's crisp intention/accident distinction misses something important about culture, which, if it exists at all, systematically produces constraints that it then hides as habit, assumption, worldview.

Kymlicka's example of an unproblematic, because unintentional, restriction on group-member rights is a native tribe that holds land in common. As Kymlicka notes, the tribe's ultimate purpose is to "provide protection against the economic and political power of the larger society to buy out or expropriate indigenous land."[3] This is an extremely important purpose: as the Dawes Act experiment demonstrated, converting reservation land to individual Indian ownership allowed white buyers and lessees to make confiscatory deals and then to move into the midst of Indian tribes, diversifying the cultural milieu in a way that was, and continues to be, devastating for tribal cultural continuity.[4] But Kymlicka vastly understates the gravity of the trade-off that holding land in common instead involves. He merely notes that tribe members "have less ability to borrow money, since they have less alienable property to use as collateral," and concludes that this is a mere "by-product" and not a "significant restriction."

The full picture of tribal common land is much more complex. Typically it will mean that most tribe members are left not with less alienable property but with none. Economically, this means not merely difficulty in finding collateral but complete abstention from the surrounding market economy. And at this point Kymlicka's failure to take note of culture's constraints becomes visible: he has not mentioned the "purpose" of promoting cultural interdependence and cohesion by blocking—for people with acute material needs—the exit marked "sell or lease your land and move away from the tribe." There is nothing to be gained by squabbling over intentions here: common ownership of land has not merely fiscal but cultural effects; and the cultural effects include constraint. Seen in this way, tribal common land seems not much different from the common property system of the Canadian Hutterite Church, which, Kymlicka concludes, does meaningfully conflict with individual autonomy.[5]

Kymlicka's sunny story of culture focuses on the ways in which it creates meaning and thus the possibility of meaningful choice.[6] Thus he regards national groups as inherently liberal if they determine membership by cultural rather than racial criteria: "[I]t is one of the tests of a liberal conception of minority rights that it defines national membership in terms of integration into a cultural community, rather than descent."[7] These are useful criteria, and do provide a conceptual zone of harmony between group rights and liberal values, but they are much more problematic in the real world than

Kymlicka acknowledges. An example that also demonstrates the way in which an exclusive focus on women's rights obscures the depth and complexity of cultural claims is the notorious Supreme Court case *Martinez v. Santa Clara Pueblo.*[8] There the tribe was charged with discriminating on the basis of sex in its membership rules, which recognized as a tribe member the child of a male member who married outside the tribe, but not the child of a female member who did the same thing. The women's rights focus on the case noted that the father of the first child was treated more favorably than the similarly situated mother of the second child. Seen from the perspective of the two children, however, the rule establishes membership based on descent, precisely what Kymlicka regards as illiberal.[9] And seen from the perspective of a young female tribe member trying to decide upon a heterosexual partner, the rule creates strong incentives for endogamy and disincentives for exogamy. To be sure, she can opt for the latter, and we could say that the rule makes her choice more meaningful. But it seems only frank to add that it makes her choice one between reward and punishment.

Cultural survival policies often focus not on women but on children. And this is no accident: raising a child in a culture—any culture—implants not only the child in the culture but the culture in the child. Kymlicka does find violations of liberal norms when religious groups withdraw their children from public schools so as to prevent them from being "tempted to leave the sect and join the wider society."[10] But this is the express goal of *all* cultural preservation policies that focus on children. As Charles Taylor has noted, Kymlicka's theory does not say why it is consistent with liberalism not merely to preserve threatened cultures for those who would claim them today, but to preserve them for "indefinite future generations" as well.[11] And as K. Anthony Appiah concludes, a program that designates future generations on the basis of their descent as the beneficiaries of cultural preservation also stipulates that they shall undergo the constraints of cultural implantation. "It seems to me not at all clear that this aim is one that we can acknowledge while respecting the autonomy of future individuals."[12]

The family is a place where illiberal things happen not only because of male superordination over women but because of adult superordination over children. This suggests that a thoroughgoing critique of the relative possibilities for the sunny and the grim stories of culture cannot be achieved with the resources of feminism alone. Cultural implantation is, moreover, inevitable: parents will always constrain their children merely by enculturating them. This suggests that dominant cultures and ethnic and national cultures within them—and, indeed, feminism too—have some very hard questions in common.

A Plea for Difficulty

MARTHA C. NUSSBAUM

*

I ADMIRE Susan Okin's essay, as I admire the entire body of her courageous and clearly argued feminist work. She states with great clarity and force the case for a critical examination of cultural practices that oppress women. She is right to say that the current liberal interest in multiculturalism holds grave dangers for women's equality. The danger is increased by the fact that issues of sex equality have rarely been seen as urgent and central by the major liberal political thinkers[1]—a sad fact that Okin's fine work over the years has done so much to diagnose, and to remedy.

But I am troubled by Okin's argument, because she makes it all sound so easy. (From now on I shall focus only on religion and not on other issues of culture.) On one side, for Okin, there are these old patriarchal religions that oppress women in keeping with sexist "founding myths." On the other side, there is the noble Enlightenment goal of a full political recognition of the equal dignity of all human beings. There is no difficulty here, other than a practical political difficulty, because religion is not seen as offering human beings anything of value. It is little more than a bag of superstitions, frequently organized around the aim of maintaining control over women. So what could be wrong with making it conform to all secular laws, including laws forbidding sex discrimination?

Far from trying to understand what might make large numbers of people in the world hold fast to religious convictions, Okin evinces contempt for religion in the very manner in which she discusses it— offhandedly, via articles in the *New York Times* (hardly a source she would regard as decisive if she were investigating women's dignity!) and via popular accounts of "founding myths" that religious people will surely find disrespectful in their casualness. (What will a Christian think of the very term "founding *myth*"? *Is* the Jewish God male? Not to many Jews, male and female, who have long since argued that the idea of God—who in any case cannot be named, and who, a fortiori, does not have a gendered name—transcends gender.[2] *Is* Islam sexist in its origins? Not to many Islamic feminists, who stress that women and men are held to share a single essential nature, and that the Koran recommends similar norms of modest conduct to both women and men.) Nor do we find any reference to the good things religion has brought into human life: its role in people's search for the ultimate meaning of life; in consoling people for the deaths of loved ones and in helping them face their own mortality; in transmitting moral values; in giving people a sense of community and civic dignity; in giving them imaginative and emotional fulfillment—and, not least, its role in many struggles for moral and political justice. If Okin were to try, for example, seriously to understand why Jews recite Psalm 99 on Shabbat—saying to God, "Your power is your love of justice"—she would then have made progress toward stating the complexity of the issue of religion's role in a liberal state.

Both Abolitionism and the U.S. civil rights movement were religious movements, and much of the contemporary struggle against racism in our nation has a religious foundation. The Indian struggle for independence and the end of caste hierarchy was inspired by Gandhi's religious ideas, which had their basis in the Gujerati Hindu tradition, as well as in Tolstoy and Ruskin. Many feminists, past and present, have been deeply religious; and this is no less true in the international women's movement. For example Ela Bhatt, founder of the Self-Employed Women's Association in India and one of the most creative feminist leaders in the developing world, views herself as a Gandhian fighter for women's independence from their "colonial" oppressor. The daughter of a Brahmin judge, she performed the sacred death ceremonies for her father, rites traditionally reserved for males. Many of the working women she organizes are also deeply religious and view religion as a support in their struggle for equality. Because Okin does not acknowledge these instances and many others like them, she cannot well describe the complexity of the issues raised by the relationship between religion and feminism.

Okin does mention the existence of "more progressive, reformed versions" of the major religions. But even this characterization is too simple. As a Reform Jew, I think that the core of Judaism is a set of timeless moral ideas that are imperfectly revealed in both text and rabbinic history. Thus "Reform," to me, does not mean a "re-formed version of" Judaism; it means a reform of defective historical practices in the direction of a more authentic (I'd say orthodox) realization of Judaism. By treating the original core of the religion as equivalent to certain patriarchal stories, Okin simply bypasses centuries of debate within each of the religions, debate highly pertinent to religion's role in the search for women's equality. For example, Reform Jews in Germany started confirming women in 1810, counted women in the minyan by 1846, abandoned asymmetrical marriage and divorce customs during the same period—somewhat in advance of secular society. My own congregation, the oldest in Chicago, voted in 1859 that "there shall be no discrimination made in favor of the male and against female worshippers." For me, these positions represent the authentic core of Judaism—as does the more recent decision to ordain women as rabbis—and we note that, again, Judaism so defined is not behind but perhaps slightly ahead of similar developments in secular society. (There are a lot more female rabbis than female members of Congress.)

Okin's approach raises practical political problems. By suggesting to religious women and men that their religion has nothing positive to contribute to the struggle for justice, and perhaps to life more generally, she alienates potential allies and thus makes her own struggle more difficult. But two arguments cast doubt on the approach at a deeper level. The first argument insists on the *intrinsic value of religious capabilities*: the ability to search for the good in a religious way is one of the liberties that is most deserving of protection by a liberal state. To say this does not entail that religious conceptions of the good are better than secular conceptions; but it does say that they are prominent among the reasonable conceptions that citizens may legitimately pursue. Given the history of religious persecution in our own nation, as in many others, it seems reasonable to give this liberty a very high degree of protection. Even if many people choose not to avail themselves of such liberties and opportunities, it is nonetheless important to leave them open for people: being able to search for the meaning of life in one's own way is a central element of a life that is fully human.

Such protections are also supported by an argument from *respect for persons*. Whereas the first argument focuses on capacity as a necessary ingredient of the human good, this one focuses on respect for what citizens actually pursue as a central ingredient of respect for them as persons. Even if one were convinced (as I suspect Okin is) that religion is all superstition, and that a comprehensive secular view of the good is correct, we do not show sufficient respect for our fellow citizens when we fail to acknowledge that they reasonably see the good differently. This is all the more true when we consider that the very content of religious convictions often states that they provide believers with fundamental elements of a view of life. So it is hard to see how we can respect the bearers of such convictions and yet not respect the choices that they make to lead traditional religious lives. It is indeed difficult to say how far the state should accommodate comprehensive religious views that seem at odds with secular liberal political values. But that is my point: it *is* difficult, rather than easy.

In short, Okin's essay raises the larger issue of the relationship between *comprehensive liberalism* and *political liberalism*.[3] Okin, to my knowledge, has never committed herself to one or the other of these forms of liberalism, but I think it is plausible to read her as endorsing a form of comprehensive liberalism, in which liberal values of autonomy and dignity pervade the fabric of the body politic, determining not only the core of the political conception but many noncore social and political matters as well.

In other words, her view resembles the views of John Stuart Mill and Joseph Raz, who see the fostering of personal autonomy in all areas of life as an appropriate goal of the state. Such moral liberals can still recognize the intrinsic worth of religious liberty and thus respect the choices of religious believers—up to a point. But, given their view that autonomous lives are better than hierarchically ordered lives, they are bound to play favorites among the religions, using the state and its persuasive apparatus to wean people away from religions that do not foster personal autonomy—as John Stuart Mill explicitly urges in *On Liberty*, where he excoriates Calvinism[4] as an "insidious ... theory of life" that creates a "pinched and hidebound type of human character." Mill holds that it is perfectly proper for public policy to be based upon the view that by teaching obedience as a good, Calvinism undermines "the desirable condition of human nature." There can be little doubt that a Millean liberal state will show public disrespect for Calvinism in all sorts of ways and will make frequent pronouncements about human flourishing and human nature that go well beyond the core of the political conception. Mill, for example, grudgingly concedes that John Knox is preferable to Alcibiades; but Pericles, he insists, is better than either one.

The *political liberal*, by contrast, begins from the fact of reasonable disagreement in society, and the existence of a reasonable plurality of comprehensive doctrines about the good, prominent among which are the religious conceptions. By calling them reasonable, the political liberal shows respect for them and commits herself to a political course that is as protective of them as it is possible to be, compatibly with a just political structure. She also shows respect for them by understanding political justification to require that the terms of cooperation should be accepted by different comprehensive views.

This form of liberalism will require all citizens to accept—not just as a modus vivendi, but on moral grounds—the core values of the political conception, among which will be the equality of all citizens. But notice that it requires endorsement of these values *as political values*, not as metaphysical values or comprehensive moral values. Thus the political liberal asks Jews and Muslims and Christians and secular humanists to accept the political equality of women as citizens, and to accept this as a salient moral fact that shapes the basic structure of society. Nonetheless, she does not ask them to accept the proposition that men and women have an equal metaphysical nature, or any other theory of human nature that some might take to ground the political claim. The claim, as John Rawls puts it, is "free-standing"—it can be hooked up in many different ways to many different comprehensive views, but it requires no particular such view for its grounding. Again, she asks citizens to endorse a *political* conception of autonomy: that is, the idea that each citizen as citizen is an equal chooser of ends, and that none should be debarred by the luck of race or sex or class from the exercise of political judgment. She asks the Calvinist to endorse this political view of autonomy as one that will be maximally protective of the spheres of life-formation that Calvinists, like other religious and nonreligious citizens, desire. But she carefully refrains from asserting that nonautonomous lives are not worth leading, or even that autonomy is a key element in the best comprehensive view of human flourishing across the board; and she carefully protects the spaces within which Calvinists and other non-Milleans can plan lives according to their own lights.

Political liberalism, the type of liberalism I would defend, seems to me far more able than comprehensive liberalism to accommodate the very great value of citizens' religious freedom. It recognizes the salience of such free searching from the very start, in the very design of its starting point; by calling the conceptions "reasonable," it gestures toward the many contributions religions have made, and continue to make, to the goodness of human life. (Satanist cults and other groups that don't seem to offer such good things have traditionally not been recognized as "religion" in American constitutional law.) Political liberalism also does better along the dimension of respect for citizens; for—ironically, since autonomy is what it is all about—comprehensive liberalism does not show very much respect for the choices citizens may make to live nonautonomously, as members of hierarchical religions or corporate bodies. Political liberalism insists that every citizen have a wide range of liberties and opportunities; so it agrees with comprehensive liberalism that a nonautonomous life should not be thrust upon someone by the luck of birth. Nonetheless, it respects such lives, given a background of liberty and opportunity, as lives that reasonable fellow citizens may pursue. In this way, it shows respect for their search for the good, where it differs from one's own, and respect for them, as reasonable.

Political liberals will be likely to judge that religion merits special deference from the liberal state, given its central importance to citizens in the search for meaning, and given the content of religious convictions, which frequently specifies their central importance and the nonoptional character of the demands they make. They will rightly be divided over the difficult issue of whether such special protection should be given to all comprehensive conceptions of the good, or only to religious conceptions. From the point of view of moral and political theory, it is difficult to justify our own tradition of free exercise jurisprudence, which singles out religion for special favor and refuses to give the same favorable treatment to Thoreau's philosophy, or to secular humanism. (This problem is mitigated, however, by the fact that such secular comprehensive views have more leeway than religion where establishment is concerned: thus the government is free to endorse environmentalism, or to celebrate Thoreau's ideas, in a way that it is not free to endorse the ideas of Judaism or Christianity.) But from a practical political standpoint it seems likely that we have two choices only: either to give religious free exercise special protection, or to give nobody any special protection. For the nonreligious comprehensive conceptions are much more likely to be personal and nontraditional, in such a way that to give them exemptions to the draft laws or the drug laws would make a mockery of such laws. While recognizing, then, that such a policy may be somewhat unfair to nonreligious comprehensive conceptions, I would favor our traditional stance of giving religion special deference, on the grounds that minority religions have been especially vulnerable in all societies and are consequently in need of this special protection.

In theory if not always in practice, our constitutional tradition has held that the state may not impose a "substantial burden" on a person's free exercise of religion, unless the state can show that this burden is in furtherance of a "compelling" government interest and is the least burdensome means of advancing that interest. More recently, the Supreme Court has departed from that tradition, holding that any neutral law of general applicability that has a rational basis may impose such burdens. The *Smith* case, which marked this change, significantly involved a substantial burden applied to a minority religion—a Native American religious group that sought exemption from the drug laws for ceremonial use of peyote. The sincerity of their religious claim was not disputed, nor was there a serious issue of public order, since they sought the exemption only for a single ceremony. Although the Court's argument in the case could be read as focusing on the question of judicial competence to adjudicate religious claims, it also showed a striking indifference to the values involved in protecting religious groups (especially minority religious groups, where this problem most frequently arises) from substantial burdens. I believe that the political liberal should be distressed at this result and should favor the approach outlined in the Religious Freedom Restoration Act of 1993, which returned to the status quo ante, requiring the government to justify any substantial burden by showing that the burden was dictated by a "compelling government interest" and was the least burdensome manner of carrying out that interest. (RFRA was passed by an overwhelming bipartisan majority but was declared unconstitutional in 1997.) Such an approach seems to show respect for religion while also insisting on the idea that the state defends a range of compelling interests that may at times bring it into conflict with religion.

I believe that this is the approach we should follow when religious practices influence the lives of women. We should ask, on the one hand, whether a proposed law (a law banning child marriage or polygamy, for example) really does impose a "substantial burden" on people's free exercise of their religion. If the answer to this question is "no," the law may go forward. I would give such a "no" answer, for example, in the case of the reform of Christian inheritance law in India, which ended unequal inheritance rights for women. The only change was the requirement that Christians treat women the way all other laws of inheritance already treated them, and the claim that this imposed a substantial burden on the freedom of Christian worship was simply implausible. If the answer is "yes," then we must look at the interests on the other side. The Indian reform of Hindu law in the 1950s, which outlawed polygamy[5] for Hindu men, probably did impose a substantial burden on the free exercise of Hindu religion, as did subsequent laws making dowry giving illegal.[6] And yet the state's interest in protecting its female citizens in fundamental areas of life (in relation to constitutional norms of sex equality and liberty) seemed to supply the state with a compelling interest in the proposed reforms. Nor, it would appear, could the state have found a less burdensome manner of achieving that compelling goal.[7]

Does sex discrimination all by itself supply the state with a compelling interest in legal change, or only discrimination that denies women certain fundamental rights? This is the most difficult issue the political liberal has to face; but she can get some help from the history of the U.S. law of religious free exercise. A classic free exercise case, *Sherbert v. Verner* (the case overruled by *Smith*) posed the question of whether mere differential treatment on the basis of religion was all by itself a substantial burden, even if the differential treatment did not do anything terribly oppressive. The Court's answer to this question was "yes." Mrs. Sherbert, a Jehovah's Witness fired because she refused to work on Saturday, was then refused state unemployment benefits because she had refused suitable employment. The Court held that despite the fact that the state might never have offered such benefits in the first place, the minute it did offer them it became a "substantial burden" if they were offered on a discriminatory basis. To deny Mrs. Sherbert, because of her religion, a benefit that others enjoyed was, the Court held, like fining someone for Saturday worship, a practice that would clearly be a "substantial burden" no matter how small the fine and how great the individual's ability to pay. So too, I think we should say, with sex discrimination: to burden women in ways that others are not so burdened is itself problematic, even if individuals are not in this way pushed into destitution.

And yet a crucial asymmetry remains: for state laws impose their burdens in a nonvoluntary manner, while religions, at least sometimes, are voluntary organizations. The religious practices of Hindus in India were rightly targeted by the secular State, because the Indian legal system makes it difficult, if not impossible, for individuals to exit from religion into the secular system, or to choose another religion. In our nation, by contrast, it seems reasonable to hold that religious organizations are voluntary. This should not prevent us from requiring religions to conform to laws by which the political conception of justice guarantees equal liberty and opportunity[8] to all adult citizens in fundamental areas of life (such as bodily integrity, health, political equality, the freedoms of speech and assembly, and the opportunity to seek employment outside the home).[9] At the same time, it seems illiberal to hold that practices internal to the conduct of the religious body itself—the choice of priests, the regulations concerning articles of clothing—must always be brought into line with a secular liberal understanding of the ultimate good. The state's interest in children as future citizens will rightly dictate some uniform educational requirements, in order to ensure that liberties and opportunities are really in place. But once they are in place, then the choices of adult citizens to remain in a religious body that refuses to hire women as priests should, I believe, be respected as a part of what we agree to respect when we acknowledge that our society contains a plurality of reasonable comprehensive conceptions of the good.

I don't like the idea of the all-male priesthood any more than Okin does. Nor do I like many of the practices of Orthodox Judaism with respect to sex equality. That is why I am a Reform Jew—and why I feel strong solidarity with Roman Catholics, female and male, who are trying to open the Church more fully to women through internal reform. But I view these attitudes as part of my own comprehensive conception of the good, which happens to be that of a Kantian Jew; I do not view that comprehensive conception as offering good reasons for state action. Such good reasons can be rightly sought only from within the core of a political conception that religious and non-religious citizens can endorse as respectful of their differing commitments. I think it is not wildly optimistic to suppose that such a core can be found, and that it will go far to protect women's vulnerability, while also protecting both women and men in their choice to worship in their own way. It will be found, however, only if we begin our search with respect for the different lives our fellow citizens choose to lead, and a sense of the complexity of our task.

PART 3

Reply

✳

SUSAN MOLLER OKIN

MANY THANKS to the respondents for their thoughtful and thought-provoking comments, many of which I agree with. Some of them extend my arguments in important ways, some of them I wish to argue against, and some of them I think indicate misperceptions of my position. Because of the last, I shall start by reiterating it briefly.

I argue that many cultures oppress some of their members, in particular women, and that they are often able to socialize these oppressed members so that they accept, without question, their designated cultural status.[1] I argue, therefore, that in the context of liberal states, when cultural or religious groups claim special rights—whether to be exercised by them together as a group or individually as members of that group—attention should be paid to the status of women within the culture or religion. This means that it is not enough for those representing the liberal state simply to listen to the requests of the self-styled group leaders. They must inquire into the point of view of the women, and to take especially seriously the perspective of the younger women.

Thus I am not arguing against freedom of religious belief, as several respondents think. Nor am I opposed to forms of multiculturalism such as educational multiculturalism, which is aimed at cross-cultural understanding and does not involve collective rights. Neither do I conclude that "feminism demands that we get rid of the offending cultures," or that we engage in "extinguishing cultures" (Bonnie Honig). I suggest, rather, that certain preconditions should obtain and discussions take place before groups are granted special rights designed to ensure the continuation of their cultures. There is a difference between urging caution about the extension of group rights and recommending the active extinction or wholesale condemnation of cultures. In most instances people exercising their individual rights will have the greatest impact on whether their culture stays the same, changes, or becomes extinct in a particular context because its members assimilate, more or less slowly, and wholly or partially, into one of the alternative cultures available, which is the kind of "becom[ing] extinct" I had in mind. As Joseph Raz, Yael Tamir, and Saskia Sassen aptly note, the potential for most cultures to change yet survive should never be underestimated. But granting group rights without paying attention to the multiple voices of members of a group may impede the kind of change from within that might otherwise occur.

Before I continue to discuss specific areas of agreement and disagreement, I want to point out that this debate is taking place only because its participants live in liberal societies, whatever the many defects of these societies. It is clear that what I have written has offended several of the respondents, but nonetheless all of our work can be published and discussed freely. In many countries, some of us would be in danger of being silenced, if not placed in physical peril, for expressing views such as we express here. And thus it seems to me somewhat odd that some respondents strike out at the liberal values that allow all of us to express ourselves on highly controversial subjects.

I shall organize my reply so as to address, in turn, two main lines of criticism, and then to engage three issues raised in some of the responses. First, some respondents are concerned that my feminism leads me to focus unnecessarily narrowly—on women and gender inequality—rather than to expand the argument to include a larger concern with human rights, socioeconomic justice, or groups other than women for whom claims to cultural group rights raise problems. The second line of criticism comes from a number of respondents who read my feminism as leading to intolerance. They think that I am hostile to or unwarrantedly critical of religions, fail to appreciate things from the perspective of "the Other," or see the views of older women in some highly patriarchal cultures as "false consciousness." Having done my best to reply to these critiques, I shall take up the discussion of religion and sex discrimination in a liberal society that Nussbaum and Sunstein initiate, engaging also the issue of religious education and the type and degree of autonomy of its citizens that I think liberalism should aim at. Finally, I shall briefly reply to Will Kymlicka, acknowledging that we share many of the same aims, though not necessarily in the same order of priority.

Recognition That the Argument Can and
Should Be Broadened

I have spent much of the past twenty-five years critiquing Western political thought and practice, including much of liberalism, past and present, from a feminist point of view.[2] Thus it is surprising to find myself depicted as "willing to accept the degree of gender equality upheld by the majority culture" (Abdullahi An-Na'im). It is not that I consider gender equality to have been achieved in liberal societies; far from it. Rather, I think that, in considering claims for group rights, liberal societies cannot reasonably expect minority cultures within them to surpass whatever level of equality between the sexes the majority culture has achieved.

Respondents such as Raz and An-Na'im ask, very reasonably, where I stand on issues such as socioeconomic inequality and social and economic human rights. As Raz suspects, I am indeed concerned about aspects of justice other than gender justice and deplore the increasing socioeconomic inequality both within and among most countries in the late twentieth century. I also agree in large part with An-Na'im on human rights, having argued that some basic social and economic rights are at least as important as many civil and political rights.[3] However, whether group self-determination is a basic human right is, clearly, complicated for me by the issue of how each group treats its own members.

Liberalism's central aim, in my view, should be to ensure that every human being has a reasonably equal chance of living a good life according to his or her unfolding views about what such a life consists in. This requires vastly more socioeconomic equality than exists in the world today. In particular, it requires that no child go without adequate food, housing, health care, or education, that no person who is sick or disabled, or who is prepared to work (including child care as work), be in need, and that governments aim at full employment, high minimum wages, and whatever redistribution of wealth is required to satisfy the needs I mention. It also requires that richer countries help poorer ones rather than, as they often now do, require of them that they cut social programs even while arming themselves expensively. I am by no means concerned only with gender equality, though I think, as do many of the respondents, that there is a particularly sharp tension between it and cultural group rights since, as I argue in my original essay, most cultures are highly gendered.

It is clear, also, in many parts of the world, including the United States, that the inequality of women and the devaluation of their unpaid work are closely linked to a great deal of poverty. Here, we can look at our own culture for a vivid example of patriarchy: a mother who is supported by a man is supposed to stay home with her young children and be economically dependent on him, but a woman without such support is excoriated for doing nothing socially useful if she takes care of her own children. In many of the world's cultures, women's substantial contributions to the maintenance of human life are so devalued that girls are often deprived of adequate food, health care, and education. Since it is by now widely known that the education of girls is the single most important factor that enables them as women to have only the number of children each wants, and that increases in mothers' incomes are much more influential on children's well-being than are increases in men's, we also know that greater equality for women will help to alleviate the stresses of overpopulation and poverty. As An-Na'im says, the advancement of various human rights around the world is crucial. However, there are many reasons to think that greater equality for women is central to this advancement.

Janet Halley, Katha Pollitt, Raz, and Tamir all want to extend the argument I make about women to other less powerful subgroups and individuals within cultures, and I appreciate and applaud their ideas. I have by no means exhausted the subject of oppression within groups that is often justified in the name of cultural preservation or religious toleration. Children, gays and lesbians, persons of minority races, disabled persons, and dissenters are all liable to varying kinds and degrees of mistreatment within many societies, including our own, and we should work to eliminate this mistreatment, in part by paying attention to those aspects of the culture that reinforce them. For example, the general level of violence that is portrayed in films and other media in the United States undoubtedly affects the level of violence—often targeted toward vulnerable persons—that actually occurs, although violence is not formally reinforced, taught as a necessary part of, or justified by, our culture.[4] (Violence against gays may be a partial exception to the last point, since homosexuality is explicitly named a sin or vice by many religious groups.)

When injustice toward or mistreatment of some people is explicitly sanctioned as necessary to a culture or religion, however, there is special cause for alarm. Raz, Honig, An-Na'im, and Bhikhu Parekh are absolutely right that no majority culture should pay less attention to its own failings than it pays to the failings of those of minorities living in its midst. But the majority has, I claim, a special responsibility to members of minority groups whose oppression it may promote or exacerbate by granting group rights without careful consideration of intragroup inequalities. As Tamir points out, the leaders of most groups are motivated to put forth their group's interests as those of a unified agent, and therefore "to foster unanimity, or at least an appearance of unanimity, even at the cost of internal oppression." Giving credence to such claims of unity by granting group rights to a nondemocratic community thus amounts to siding with those in power, the privileged against the marginalized, the traditionalists against the reformers, who often portray dissent as disloyalty to the group. When Parekh enjoins liberalism to "engage in an open-minded dialogue with other doctrines and cultures," including illiberal ones, he does not confront the difficulty this poses when the self-proclaimed leaders of a cultural group are in no way representative of all or even most of its members.

Defense of My Feminist Critique of the Patriarchy of Most Religions and Cultures

While many respondents agree that almost all cultures and religions are more or less patriarchal, several claim that the few remarks I make about the founding myths of Judaism, Christianity, and Islam portray them as more patriarchal than is warranted. To some of this critique, it is difficult even to begin to respond. Nussbaum presents the most sex-egalitarian aspects of Reform Judaism as "authentic," even "orthodox" Judaism, with all the other past or present manifestations of Judaism relegated to the status of "defective historical practices."[5] Though she thinks I show contempt for religion by citing articles in the *New York Times* and founding myths as evidence about religious ideas and practices, for her extraordinary depiction of Judaism she cites very little evidence at all.

Azizah al-Hibri, far more credible on the issue of origins, points out that the earliest texts in Islam were considerably more woman-friendly than later interpretations of texts and laws have been. This leads to the possibility of the exciting types of reinterpretation of Islam that scholars such as she and An-Na'im pursue.[6] But her attempt to present contemporary Islam as relatively sex-egalitarian and open-minded is unconvincing. *Undoubtedly* it is the task of Muslims to reinterpret Islamic jurisprudence, but surely it must have taken more than the "several jurists" she mentions to make Muslim law in so many parts of the world today so patriarchal—with polygamy for men only, unequal divorce laws, unfair laws about rape and adultery, and in some countries women and even young girls forced to cover themselves completely or be arrested or beaten. When al-Hibri writes that "each Muslim, male or female, is guaranteed his or her freedom of conscience," this may indeed be the teaching of the Qur'an, but it is surely not practiced in the countries where apostasy is a crime for Muslims and converting a Muslim to some other religion is a capital offense.

Reading Nussbaum's and al-Hibri's criticisms of me for not paying sufficient attention to the ways in which Judaism and Islam are compatible with feminism, I cannot but wonder whose argument it really is that, as al-Hibri puts it, renders the "inessential Other . . . remarkably indistinguishable and voiceless," drowning her out by the dominant "I"? I think of a Malaysian Muslim woman I met at a recent international conference who responded to my question about feminists in the West who defend polygamy by saying, amazed and heatedly: "*No woman* likes polygamy!"[7] I recall an Indonesian Muslim woman at the same conference who said, in response to my discussion of ways in which Muslim women's rights groups are working for change in the Muslim world: "How can they hope to succeed? There are more than twenty million illiterate Muslim women in Indonesia, and they know their rights: they know that if they do not obey their husbands, they will go to hell." Am I the silencer of such voices, in taking into account that hundreds of millions of women are rendered voiceless or virtually so by the male-dominated religions with which they live? Or are the silencers those feminists who downplay the patriarchy of many variants of their religions, but who enjoy every moment of their own lives freedoms that are unthinkable to those "Others" whose voices they think I am drowning out? Of course it is good that pro-religion feminists are seeking out and trying to foster the most woman-friendly strands within their own religions. But to do this does not entail denying or even downplaying the dominant patriarchal strands that have so long prevailed within them.

Bonnie Honig presents five counterexamples to demonstrate that the three major Western religions are "less univocally patriarchal" than I suggest, but none of them helps to build her case. First, she points out that the religions' control of women's sexuality is "usually matched" by efforts to control men's. However, this is not accurate. As an example, think of the far harsher punishments that women have received, under all three religions, for adultery, or the fact that Muslim polygamy is and Jewish polygamy was (and in isolated groups still is) for men only. (One of the suggestions put forth by Taslima Nasrin—the radical Bangladeshi Muslim feminist forced to flee her country—that was considered most outrageous was that Muslim women should be permitted to have several husbands.) Also, the control of men's sexuality often affects *women*'s religious status more than men's. For example, because of the prohibition against sexual arousal during worship, Orthodox Jews segregate by sex, and in some branches women may not pray aloud, for even their voices are "considered sexual organs" that might arouse men while they pray.[8] A less patriarchal religion might have concluded that the solution to the problem was for women to play the central roles in worship. Honig finishes her first point by citing nuns as "a stunning exception" to my statement that traditions and cultures often make it virtually impossible for women to live independently of men. But she does not note that nuns live within the rule of an all-male hierarchy and cannot celebrate the most fundamental sacrament of their religion, the Eucharist, without a priest.

Second, countering my point that the three major Western religions place undue stress on the reproductive role of fathers, neglecting that of mothers by comparison, Honig notes that Judaism is passed on matrilineally. However, she neglects to mention that, within Orthodoxy, a woman's ability to pass on her Judaism is substantially controlled by men. She must be married to an Orthodox Jew to be able to have children considered legitimate and Orthodox, and she can be divorced by him in a way that leaves her, though not him, unfree to remarry and have legitimate Orthodox children. Third, on the same issue, Honig cites the virgin birth of Jesus as "attenuat[ing] the role of the father in reproduction." But why has Jesus been of such importance for two millennia? Because of who his mother was? Or because of who Christians believe his Father was? After all, only God the Father made the "virgin birth" possible.

Fourth, Honig suggests that veiling can be an "empowering practice" for many Muslim feminists, who are able to move from country to city and go out to work as a result of it. I do not doubt that this is so. But surely to be unable to go out and practice one's profession without being enshrouded from head to toe is not, on the whole, an empowering situation in which to live, unless it is a temporary transition to greater freedom. Finally, against my point that polygamy often makes women more vulnerable within marriage, Honig cites a case where the first three wives of a French immigrant were placed, by being co-wives, in "a situation of solidarity." But she does not explain why, if polygamy is so empowering to wives, the issue about which they banded together was precisely . . . more polygamy! Their collective resistance to their husband's adding yet another, younger wife to the household may have been one of the only interests they had in common.

Another issue on which a couple of the commentators find me unduly intolerant of the practices of others is clitoridectomy. But both Sander Gilman and Parekh—though the latter clearly condemns its being performed on children—seem not to realize that clitoridectomy has devastating consequences for women's sexuality. The male equivalent, from the point of view of sexual (as opposed to reproductive) functioning, would be "penidectomy"—that is to say the removal of all, or at least most, of the penis.[9] Thus Gilman's lengthy preoccupation with the lessening of male sexual pleasure that might possibly result from circumcision is completely beside the point. He takes "[t]he question of pleasure" to be entirely culturally relative, asking rhetorically, "Is it not clear that even sexual pleasure is as much a reflex of the mind as of the body!" But if had consulted just a few women, he could easily have found out that there are limits to the power of the mind. Without a clitoris, a woman cannot experience orgasm, any more than a man could without a penis. Moreover, it is clear from a number of the statements I quote from African women that the *purpose* of clitoridectomy is to take the pleasure out of sex for women, in order to preserve their virginity before marriage and their fidelity within it. Thus, to Parekh's question about sane, adult women who wish to freely undergo clitoridectomy after the birth of their last children, as a way of regulating their sexuality, to be mothers foremost and wives only secondarily, or as a form of religious sacrifice, I suggest: respond to her just as one would to a father who wanted his penis amputated for any of these reasons. Before heading off to the surgeon, go and talk to a psychiatrist or a marriage counselor.

To conclude this section, I wish to respond to several commentators who raise the thorny issue, mentioned only briefly in my essay, of how a feminist outsider should respond when women—especially older women—subordinated within a culture have no complaints about their circumstances and even help to reproduce them. Robert Post, for example, suggests that Orthodox Ashkenazi Jewish women might well not view themselves as disadvantaged within their religion—rather, despite their very distinct roles, seeing themselves as having equal dignity with men. (Something like "separate but equal"?) But isn't this the type of Judaism that not only "disqualifies women from important religious rituals" (as Post notes), but in which the birth and coming-of-age of boys (but not girls) are celebrated with important rituals, women have to be ritually cleansed after each menstrual period before they and their husbands can have sexual intercourse, and men thank God every morning that they are not women? (Imagine for a moment a religious group whose lighter-skinned members thanked God every morning for not giving them darker skin.) My view is that, however certain such women are of the *rightness* of their role within such a context, surely they would be seriously deluded in viewing themselves as having "equal dignity" with men.

Addressing the same issue, Parekh regards it as "patronizing, even impertinent" to regard some of the women who do not "share the feminist view" as "victims of a culturally generated false consciousness." But he goes on to say that "sometimes they are [brainwashed]," which seems a rather more blunt expression of the same point. One need not rely on the Marxist theory of false consciousness to recognize that persons subjected to unjust conditions often adapt their preferences so as to conceal the injustice of their situation from themselves. Liberals from John Stuart Mill to Jon Elster, Amartya Sen, Cass Sunstein, Uma Narayan, and Martha Nussbaum have written of such adaptation.[10] It is largely the importance of this issue that leads to my conviction that any proposal for cultural group rights should both include the younger women of the group and explore carefully claims that certain practices are crucial to "being a woman" within the culture. As the debate over head scarves in France showed, not only do young women tend to be the focus of intercultural disputes and to have most at stake in the outcomes, but they are often at odds with each other—some viewing their cultural practices or insignia as positive statements of their identity, others seeing such things as imposed on them by their families or cultural leaders.

The average older woman raised in any patriarchal culture is less likely to want change, for several reasons. It is not easy to question cultural constraints that have had a major impact on one's whole life. If one has had to adapt one's preferences and conceptions of self to please men and accept one's social role as subordinate to them, such adaptation is not easily changed. Moreover, the experience of such constraints may produce a psychological need to enforce them on the younger generation. Furthermore, an older woman's relatively high status within the group (as Parekh suggests) results in part from her leading a virtuous life, which includes successful enculturation of her children and grandchildren into their prescribed gender roles. Also, in some cultures the main experience of power a woman ever gains, as she ages, is power over her daughters-in-law.[11] So I emphasize the importance of listening to the young women of a minority culture regulated by patriarchal norms not out of an impulse to "divide and rule," as Homi Bhabha suggests, but rather because I recognize the importance of hearing the very " 'local' leavenings of liberty" and indigenous feminist voices that he thinks I want to obscure.

LIMITS ON RELIGIOUS FREEDOM WITHIN A LIBERAL STATE?

Not only do various respondents object that I portray the major Western as well as other religions too patriarchally. Some more reasonably demand that I subject domestic practices within liberal states to the same degree of scrutiny to which I am subjecting "foreign" or imported practices. Nussbaum and Sunstein make challenging arguments about the specific issue of whether religious freedom should trump sex discrimination or vice versa. Thus it is important that I address group rights issues that have developed from the seemingly individual rights inscribed in the First Amendment to the United States Constitution. The free exercise clause, in particular, has been interpreted as a group right, enabling religious institutions to be exempt from certain generally applicable laws, including laws against sex discrimination. Nussbaum is absolutely right that this is a difficult issue. It is difficult because freedom of religion is clearly inscribed in the Constitution, because sex discrimination now conflicts with many laws and has been recognized as in many cases unconstitutional, and because, as I have argued, so much of the practice and belief of some religions commonly practiced in the United States runs counter to gender equality. Nussbaum argues that the protection of religion has not extended far enough, especially since the Supreme Court's 1990 decision prohibiting the use of peyote, an illegal drug, for religious purposes.[12] Because of the special emphasis that she thinks should be placed on religious freedom, she favors the approach taken in the Religious Freedom Restoration Act (subsequently ruled unconstitutional). This would require that any law placing a substantial burden on a religious group be dictated by a "compelling government interest." Though at first concluding that this would disallow religiously based sex discrimination, she then appeals to the voluntary nature of religious membership in our society, to conclude that, so long as the liberties and opportunities of children are ensured by their education, society should then respect the rights of adult citizens to join or remain in religious bodies that exclude women from certain religious functions, such as the Catholic priesthood.

Cass Sunstein too sees the issue as potentially very controversial yet concludes differently. He doubts strongly that the option of exit is sufficient to justify sex discriminatory religious practices, because the kinds of internalized subordination that girls and women experience in many religions are likely to render them "unable to scrutinize the practices with which they have grown up," and because of the effects of such toleration of female exclusion or subordination on other women. Sunstein points out that frequently the interest in getting rid of sex discrimination can be far stronger than our interest in any particular crime or tort, for which a religious group *can* be held responsible; thus the current asymmetry that treats the conflict between the two types of law and religion differently is invalid. Fully aware that the requirement of sex equality "would go toward the heart of religious convictions," he notes that some other aspects of criminal and civil law do so also. Moreover, to the extent that sex equality conflicts with religion, "it is a contingent, time-bound, highly empirical fact, one that bears little on the question of principle from the liberal point of view." He concludes that no line should be drawn between other aspects of law and the laws against sex discrimination. Rather, the liberal state should assess, in the case of each relevant law, how great an intrusion or heavy a burden the law would place on religious institutions, and how legitimate or strong the justification for imposing it.

I am generally very sympathetic to Sunstein's conclusion, yet I have three comments to make on it. First, if a religious group wished to continue its sex discriminatory practices, under the Sunstein ruling it would have a vested interest in showing that sex discrimination was at the very heart of its beliefs. This, on the one hand, may entrench sex discrimination within certain religious groups. On the other hand, its being spelled out loud and clear would make existing and potential members well aware of it. Second, Sunstein's solution requires that courts rule on the centrality or peripheral nature of various doctrinal matters—which they have generally tried to avoid doing.[13] Third, agreeing more with Sunstein than with Nussbaum about the voluntariness of religious beliefs, I think that there is an even clearer case for prohibiting sex discrimination in the educational practices of religious groups than in practices opted into by adults who are aware of alternative ways of life.

Nussbaum asks whether I am a political liberal—like Rawls—or a comprehensive liberal (some would say "autonomy liberal")—like Mill and Raz. The liberalism I subscribe to requires that children's education not leave them with knowledge only of their parents' culture or religion, much less that it give them the impression that that is the only "right" way to live. But this does not place me neatly within either category. As I shall explain, I subscribe to a position in between. Even the most prominent "political liberal" of all, John Rawls, who rejects the imposition on religious sects that "oppose the modern world" of the requirement that their children be educated so as to value autonomy and individuality, also argues that the liberal state should require that all children be educated so as to be self-supporting and be informed of their rights as citizens, including freedom of conscience. He argues this even though he recognizes that the effect of this may in some cases lead to comprehensive liberalism.[14] Nussbaum, who also endorses political liberalism, says that, while it respects nonautonomous lives, it "insists that every citizen have a wide range of liberties and opportunities; so it agrees . . . that a nonautonomous life should not be thrust upon someone by the luck of birth." This leads her to require that children's education ensure such liberties and opportunities. As I understand her, despite her claim to being a political liberal, Nussbaum thus places herself between the camps of comprehensive and political liberals. Many parents belonging to religions or cultures that do not respect autonomy would (and do) very strongly resist their children's being exposed to any religious or cultural views but their own. But, like Nussbaum (and to a lesser extent Rawls) I do not think that liberal states should allow this to happen. I believe that a certain degree of nonautonomy should be available as an option to a mature adult with extensive knowledge of other options, but not thrust on a person by his or her parents or group, through indoctrination—including sexist socialization—and lack of exposure to alternatives. But such hybrid liberalism puts strict limits on the extent to which children's education can be confined within the framework of any single religion, and prohibits it from being sex discriminatory in any way.

The question that remains is what must education be like, for religious affiliations to be as voluntary as possible? Given that it is central to most religions that their members try to pass on their beliefs to their children, it would strike an intolerable blow at religion not to allow this to take place. But it seems not at all unreasonable, within the context of a liberal state that values its citizens' capacity to make informed decisions about whether to lead autonomous or nonautonomous lives as adults, to require both that children's education—including their religious education—be nonsexist, and that all children be thoroughly exposed to and taught about other religious as well as secular beliefs held by people around the world. Indeed, without this, it would be difficult to claim that their adhering to their parents' religion was voluntary at all. In the United States, the establishment clause has led to such a separation of church and state that, constitutionally at any rate, no religion is supposed to be taught in the public schools. Yet at the same time, parents are permitted to send their children to private schools that teach one religion as the only truth, or to home school them in such beliefs. However, surely there is a distinction between "teaching religion" and "teaching about religion." The latter takes place in the public schools in a number of liberal nation-states that do not have established churches. Here in the United States, the study of comparative religion could, and I argue should, be taught to all young people. It is, after all, an important part of history, a subject about which most of our high school (and even many of our college) graduates are now pitifully ignorant, and that, if well taught, is inevitably controversial, even without a significant component on the history of religions.[15] This innovation may well be resisted by parents who believe strongly that their own faiths are the whole and the only truth, as well perhaps as by parents who do not want their children taught about religion at all. But without some knowledge of various religious beliefs and practices, as well as secular ones, children's basic liberties to think about their own lives and decide what is best for them seem unduly truncated.

TOWARD A FEMINIST, MORE EGALITARIAN MULTICULTURALISM

Finally, I agree with Will Kymlicka's important observation that multiculturalism and feminism are, in some ways, related struggles. Both seek the recognition of difference in the context of norms that are universal in theory, but not in practice. Still, an essential difference remains. The few special rights that women claim qua women do not give more powerful women the right to control less powerful women. In contrast, cultural group rights do often (in not-so-obvious ways) reinforce existing hierarchies. As Kymlicka indicates, he and I share this concern, though he tends to prioritize cultural group rights and I, as is by now obvious, prioritize women's equality. What we need to strive toward is a form of multiculturalism that gives the issues of gender and other intragroup inequalities their due—that is to say, a multiculturalism that effectively treats all persons as each other's moral equals.

NOTES

*

SUSAN MOLLER OKIN
IS MULTICULTURALISM BAD FOR WOMEN?

Thanks to Elizabeth Beaumont for research assistance and to Beaumont and Joshua Cohen for helpful comments on an earlier draft.

1. *International Herald Tribune*, 2 February 1996, News section.

2. Will Kymlicka, *Multicultural Citizenship: A Liberal Theory of Minority Rights* (Oxford: Oxford University Press, 1995), pp. 89, 76. See also Kymlicka, *Liberalism, Community, and Culture* (Oxford: The Clarendon Press, 1989). It should be noted that Kymlicka himself does not argue for extensive or permanent group rights for those who have voluntarily immigrated.

3. Avishai Margalit and Moshe Halbertal, "Liberalism and the Right to Culture," *Social Research* 61, 3 (Fall 1994): 491.

4. For example, Chandran Kukathas, "Are There Any Cultural Rights?," *Political Theory* 20, 1 (1992): 105–39.

5. Okin, "Feminism and Multiculturalism: Some Tensions," *Ethics* 108, 4 (July 1998): 661–84.

6. For example, Kymlicka, *Liberalism, Community, and Culture* and *Multicultural Citizenship* (esp. chap. 8). Kymlicka does not apply his requirement that groups be internally liberal to those he terms "national minorities," but I will not address that aspect of his theory here.

7. See, for example, Kirti Singh, "Obstacles to Womens' Rights in India," in *Human Rights of Women: National and International Perspectives*, ed. Rebecca J. Cook (Philadephia: University of Pennsylvania Press, 1994), pp. 375–96, esp. pp. 378–89.

8. I cannot discuss here the roots of this male preoccupation, except to say (following feminist theorists Dorothy Dinnerstein, Nancy Chodorow, Jessica Benjamin, and, before them, Jesuit anthropologist Walter Ong) that it seems to have a lot to do with female primary parenting. It is also clearly related to the uncertainty of paternity, which technology has now counteracted. If these issues are at the root of it, then the cultural preoccupation with controlling women is not an inevitable fact of human life but a contingent factor that feminists have a considerable interest in changing.

9. See, for example, Arvind Sharma, ed., *Women in World Religions* (Albany: SUNY Press, 1987); John Stratton Hawley, ed., *Fundamentalism and Gender* (Oxford: Oxford University Press, 1994).

10. See Carol Delaney, *Abraham on Trial: The Social Legacy of Biblical Myth* (Princeton: Princeton University Press, 1998). Note that in the Qur'anic version, it is not Isaac but Ishmael whom Abraham prepares to sacrifice.

11. *New York Times*, 5 October 1996, A4. The role that older women in such cultures play in perpetuating these practices is important but complex and cannot be addressed here.

12. *New York Times*, 26 June 1997, A9.

13. *International Herald Tribune*, 2 February 1996, News section.

14. *New York Times*, 12 March 1997, A8.

15. This practice is discussed in Henry S. Richardson, *Practical Reasoning about Final Ends* (Cambridge: Cambridge University Press, 1994), esp. pp. 240–43, 262–63, 282–84.

16. *Agence France Presse*, 18 May 1997, International News section.

17. See, however, Bhikhu Parekh's "Minority Practices and Principles of Toleration," *International Migration Review* (April 1996): 251–84, in which he directly addresses and critiques a number of cultural practices that devalue the status of women.

18. Sebastian Poulter, "Ethnic Minority Customs, English Law, and Human Rights," *International and Comparative Law Quarterly* 36, 3 (1987): 589–615.

19. Amy Gutmann, "The Challenge of Multiculturalism in Political Ethics," *Philosophy and Public Affairs* 22, 3 (Summer 1993): 171–204.

20. Mahnaz Afkhami, ed., *Faith and Freedom: Women's Human Rights in the Muslim World* (Syracuse: Syracuse University Press, 1995); Valentine M. Moghadam, ed., *Identity Politics and Women: Cultural Reassertions and Feminisms in International Perspective* (Boulder, CO: Westview Press, 1994); Susan Moller Okin, "Culture, Religion, and Female Identity Formation" (unpublished manuscript, 1997).

21. For one of the best and most recent accounts of this, and for legal citations for the cases mentioned below, see Doriane Lambelet Coleman, "Individualizing Justice through Multiculturalism: The Liberals' Dilemma," *Columbia Law Review* 96, 5 (1996): 1093–1167.

22. *New York Times*, 2 December 1996, A6.

23. See Coleman, "Individualizing Justice through Multiculturalism."

24. See, for example, Nilda Rimonte, "A Question of Culture: Cultural Approval of Violence against Women in the Asian-Pacific Community and the Cultural Defense," *Stanford Law Review* 43 (1991): 1311–26.

25. Kymlicka, *Liberalism, Community, and Culture*, p. 165.

26. Ibid., pp. 168–72, 195–98.

27. Kymlicka, *Multicultural Citizenship*, p. 92.

28. Kymlicka, *Liberalism, Community, and Culture*, pp. 171–72.

29. Kymlicka, *Multicultural Citizenship*, pp. 153, 165.

30. See, for example, Amartya Sen, "More Than One Hundred Million Women Are Missing," *New York Review of Books*, 20 December 1990.

31. Will Kymlicka, *Contemporary Political Philosophy: An Introduction* (Oxford: The Clarendon Press, 1990), pp. 239–62.

32. *New York Times*, 12 October 1996, A6. Similar views were expressed on National Public Radio.

BONNIE HONIG
"MY CULTURE MADE ME DO IT"

1. Leila Ahmed, *Women and Gender in Islam: Historical Roots of a Modern Debate* (New Haven: Yale University Press, 1992), pp. 223–24.

AZIZAH Y. AL-HIBRI
IS WESTERN PATRIARCHAL FEMINISM GOOD FOR
THIRD WORLD / MINORITY WOMEN?

1. Okin, this volume, p. 11.

2. Ibid., p. 22.

3. Ibid., pp. 13–14. For people of faith, Okin's "founding myths" are not myths at all.

4. Qur'an, 4:1; 59:13.

5. Ibid., 2:35–36.

6. For more on patriarchal interpretations affecting women, see my "Islam, Law and Custom," *American University Journal of International Law and Policy* 12, 1 (1997): 1–44.

7. For a discussion of how Orientalist colonialist attitude affected various populations, especially women, see Rana Kabbani, *Imperial Fictions* (London: Pandora, 1994), esp. preface to New Edition. See also Marnia Lazreg, *The Eloquence of Silence* (New York: Routledge, 1994), esp. chaps. 1–3 and 6.

8. Okin, this volume, pp. 9–10, 14–15.

9. For more on this, see my "Islamic Constitutionalism and the Concept of Democracy," *Case Western Reserve Journal of International Law* 24, 1 (1992): 1–27, esp. 4–7, 21–24.

10. For more on Muslim women *mujtahids* (i.e., those who engage in *ijtihad*), see my "Islamic Law and Muslim Women in America," in *One Nation under God? Religion and American Culture*, ed. Marjorie Garber and Rebecca L. Walkowitz (New York: Routledge, 1999).

11. Al-Hibri, "Islamic Constitutionalism and the Concept of Democracy," pp. 6–7. See also al-Hibri, "Islam, Law and Custom," pp. 6–7.

12. Qur'an, 49:13

13. Al-Hibri, "Islam, Law and Custom," pp. 6–7.

14. For an excellent discussion of this phenomenon, see the article by David Smolin, "Will International Human Rights Be Used as a Tool of Cultural Geno-

cide? The Interaction of Human Rights Norms, Religion, Culture and Gender," *Journal of Law and Religion* 12, 1 (1995–96): 143–71.

15. Ibid., pp. 165–67.

16. Ibid., p. 165.

17. Okin, this volume, p. 21.

18. Ibid., p. 24.

19. Ibid., p. 21.

20. All personal status codes in Muslim countries recognize the right of the wife to judicial divorce for reason of harm. Some countries defined harm specifically to include verbal abuse. For more on this, see al-Hibri, "Islam, Law and Culture,"p. 13 n. 58. Furthermore, traditional jurists, such as the tenth-century jurist Ibn Hazm, have whole chapters on the punishment of *Qisas*. *Qisas* punishments are based on the biblical/Qur'anic principle of "an eye for an eye." They are applied only in specific kinds of crimes when the victim declines to forgive or accept monetary damages. See al-Hibri, "The Muslim Perspective on the Clergy-Penitent Privilege," *Loyola of Los Angeles Law Review* 29 (June 1996): 1726–30. For example, according to Ibn Hazm, a man who intentionally harms a woman (even if she is his wife) by causing a tear to the opening of her vagina will be punished by the infliction on him of a similar tear in the corresponding area of his body. Ibn Hazm, *Al-Muhalla Bi al-Athar* (Beirut: Dar al-Kutub al-'Ilmiyah; reprint, 1988), 11:88. Numerous other types of injuries and punishments are detailed in Ibn Hazm's chapter on *Qisas*.

21. On this point, see, e.g., Ibn Hazm, *Al-Isal fi al-Muhalla Bi al-Athar*, pp. 8, 423–24 (quoting and commenting on Qur'anic verse 3:104, which enjoins Muslims to promote the good and prohibit evil).

22. Ibid.

23. Qur'an, 3:104.

24. For more on this point, see, e.g., Taha Jabir al 'Alwani, *The Ethics of Disagreement in Islam*, 2d ed. (The International Institute of Islamic Thought, 1996), esp. pp. 91–107.

25. For one account of this incident, see Subhi Mahmassani, *Al-Awda' al-Tashri'iyah Fi al-Duwal al-Arabiyah*, 3d ed. (Beirut: Dar al-'Ilm li al-Malayin, ed. 1965), p. 159.

YAEL TAMIR
SIDING WITH THE UNDERDOGS

1. I have developed this argument is greater detail in "Against Collective Rights," in *Multicultural Questions*, ed. Christian Joppke and Steven Lukes (Oxford: Oxford University Press, 1999).

2. Charles Taylor, "The Politics of Recognition,' in *Multiculturalism*, ed. Amy Gutmann (Princeton: Princeton University Press, 1994), pp. 58–59 (my emphasis).

3. Will Kymlicka, *Liberalism, Community, and Culture* (Oxford: The Clarendon Press, 1989), p. 149.

4. Ibid.

SANDER L. GILMAN
"BARBARIC" RITUALS?

1. Paolo Mantegazza, *The Sexual Relations of Mankind*, trans. Samuel Putnam (New York: Eugenics Publishing Company, 1938), p. 99.

2. Susannah Heschel, "Jüdisch-feministiche Theologie und Antijudaismus in christlich-feministicher Theologie," in *Verdrängte Vergangenheit, die uns bedrängt: Feministische Theologie in der Verantwortung für die Geschichte*, ed. Leonore Siegele-Wenschkewitz (Munich: Chr. Kaiser, 1988), pp. 54–103.

3. Humphrey Carpenter, *A Serious Character: The Life of Ezra Pound* (Boston: Houghton Mifflin), p. 362.

4. Gabriel Groddeck, *De Judaeis praeputium attrahentibus ad illustrandum locum I, Cor. VII. 18* (Leipzig, 1690), reprinted in *Horae hebraicae et Talmudicae*, ed. Christianus Schoettgenius (Dresden: Thomam Fritsch, 1733), p. 1163 (flesh); p. 1166 (small number of Jews).

5. Edward O. Laumann, Christopher M. Masi, and Ezra W. Zuckerman, "Circumcision in the United States: Prevalence, Prophylactic Effects, and Sexual Practice," *Journal of the American Medical Association* 277 (1997): 1052–57.

6. J. R. Taylor, A. P. Lockwood, and A. J. Taylor, "The Prepuce: Specialized Mucosa of the Penis and Its Loss to Circumcision," *British Journal of Urology* 77 (1996): 291–95.

7. Helene Deutsch, *The Therapeutic Process, the Self, and Female Psychology: Collected Psychoanalytic Papers*, ed. Paul Roazen (New Brunswick, NJ: Transaction Publishers, 1993), pp. 49–61.

ABDULLAHI AN-NA'IM
PROMISES WE SHOULD ALL KEEP
IN COMMON CAUSE

1. See Abdullahi A. An-Na'im and Francis M. Deng, eds., *Human Rights in Africa: Cross-Cultural Perspectives* (Washington, DC: Brookings Institution, 1990); and Abdullahi A. An-Na'im, ed., *Human Rights in Cross-Cultural Perspectives: Quest for Consensus* (Philadelphia: University of Pennsylvania Press, 1992).

2. Other sources include the African Charter of Human and Peoples Rights of 1981, the ILO Conventions of 1957 and 1989, as well as the European Framework Convention of 1995.

ROBERT POST
BETWEEN NORMS AND CHOICES

1. Will Kymlicka, *Multicultural Citizenship: A Liberal Theory of Minority Rights* (Oxford: Oxford University Press, 1995), p. 36.
2. Ibid., p. 84.
3. Ibid., p. 7.
4. Ibid., p. 194.
5. Ibid., p. 36.

SASKIA SASSEN
CULTURE BEYOND GENDER

1. I discuss this literature in "Toward a Feminist Analytics of the Global Economy," in Saskia Sassen, *Globalization and Its Discontents: Essays on the Mobility of People and Money* (New York: The New Press, 1998).
2. See, for instance, "Whose City Is It? Globalization and the Formation of New Claims," in Sassen, *Globalization and Its Discontents*.

HOMI K. BHABHA
LIBERALISM'S SACRED COW

1. *New York Times*, 18 November 1998, A7.

CASS R. SUNSTEIN
SHOULD SEX EQUALITY LAW APPLY
TO RELIGIOUS INSTITUTIONS?

I am grateful to Joshua Cohen, Catharine MacKinnon, and Martha Nussbaum for valuable comments on an earlier draft.

1. Of course there can be tensions between minority cultures and other equality concerns, for example the interest in racial equality; I restrict my discussion to sex equality here.
2. The term "religious institutions" can cover many things—from churches and temples themselves, to religious schools, to private sphere employers who act on their religious convictions. I am deliberately leaving the term vague here.
3. American law makes the basic prohibitions on employment discrimination inapplicable where religion, sex, or national origin is "a bona fide occupational qualification reasonably necessary to the normal operation of that particular business or enterprise." 42 U.S.C. 2000e-2(e). The prohibition is generally inapplicable "to a religious corporation, association, educational institution, or society with respect to the employment of individuals of a particular religion to perform

work connected with the carrying on by such corporation, association, educational institution, or society of its activities." 42 USC 2000e-1.

4. Of course the American Constitution applies only to the state, and not to private institutions; hence the asymmetry thesis has its force when government goes beyond the Constitution to apply a prohibition on sex discrimination to most private institutions but not to religion.

5. See *EEOC v. Catholic University of America*, 856 F. Supp. 1 (DDC 1994), affirmed, 83 F.2d 455 (DC Cir. 1994).

6. *Bollard v. California Province of the Society of Jesus*, 1998 U.S. Dist. LEXIS 7563 (15 May 1998).

7. See the discussion in Okin, *supra*.

8. See, e.g., *Young v. Northern Illinois Conference of United Methodist Church*, 21 F.3d 184 (7th Cir. 1994).

9. *EEOC v. Catholic University of America*, 83 F.3d 455 (DC Cir. 1994).

10. To say this is not to deny that norms of sex equality are often an outgrowth of religious beliefs as well, nor is it to offer a general view about whether the world's religions promote or deny sex equality; it is doubtful that any general view would make much sense.

11. See Cass R. Sunstein, *Free Markets and Social Justice* (Oxford: Oxford University Press, 1997), chaps. 1 and 2.

12. Employment Division, *Department of Human Services v. Smith*, 494 U.S. 872 (1990). Technically, *Smith* holds that a facially neutral law will be upheld so long as it has a "rational basis," unless it is discriminatorily motivated. The Court did not overrule *Sherbert v. Verner*, 374 U.S. 398 (1963) (holding that a state may not deny unemployment benefits to a Seventh-Day Adventist who was fired because she would not work on Saturday) or *Wisconsin v. Yoder*, 406 U.S. 205 (1972) (allowing Amish teenagers to be exempted from a requirement of school attendance until the age of sixteen); but it did read those cases extremely narrowly. It should be noted that the Smith decision was surprising as well as controversial, and that it remains an object of continuing debate, not only in political and academic circles but also within the Supreme Court itself.

13. In *EEOC v. Catholic University of America*, 83 F.3d 455 (DC Cir. 1994), the court held, without much explanation, that *Smith* did not undermine previous holdings that there was an exception for ministers from the general sex discrimination law.

JOSEPH RAZ
HOW PERFECT SHOULD ONE BE?
AND WHOSE CULTURE IS?

1. For my own views, see "Multiculturalism: A Liberal Perspective," in *Ethics in the Public Domain: Essays in the Morality of Law and Politics*, rev. ed. (Oxford: Oxford University Press, 1995).

JANET E. HALLEY
CULTURE CONSTRAINS

1. Will Kymlicka, *Multicultural Citizenship: A Liberal Theory of Minority Rights* (Oxford: Oxford University Press, 1995).

2. Ibid., pp. 35–44.

3. For Kymlicka's analysis of this case, see ibid., pp. 43–44.

4. See D. S. Otis, *The Dawes Act and the Allotment of Indian Lands* (Norman: University of Oklahoma Press, 1973), esp. pp. 93, 115, 119, and 124–55.

5. Kymlicka, *Multicultural Citizenship*, p. 161, discussing *Hofer v. Hofer*, 13 DLR (3d) 1 (1970).

6. Kymlicka, *Multicultural Citizenship*, pp. 82–92.

7. Ibid., p. 23. In the past Kymlicka did acknowledge this range of problems associated with common land—see his book *Liberalism, Community, and Culture* (Oxford: The Clarendon Press, 1989), pp. 144–46 and 197—but his more recent defense of cultural rights omits them.

8. 436 U.S. 49, 98 S.Ct. 1670 (1977). The Supreme Court held that the tribe had sovereign immunity from suit under the Indian Civil Rights Act and dismissed all claims against the individual defendant on grounds that the ICRA did not create a private cause of action upon which the plaintiffs could sue.

9. The tribe's rule also prohibited the second child from ever being naturalized as a member of the tribe. 98 S.Ct. at 1674.

10. Kymlicka, *Multicultural Citizenship*, pp. 41–42.

11. Charles Taylor, "The Politics of Recognition," in *Multiculturalism and the Politics of Recognition*, ed. Amy Gutmann (Princeton: Princeton University Press, 1994), pp. 25–73, 40–41 n. 16.

12. K. Anthony Appiah, "Identity, Authenticity, Survival: Multicultural Societies and Social Reproduction," in Gutmann, *Multiculturalism*, pp. 149–63, 157.

MARTHA C. NUSSBAUM
A PLEA FOR DIFFICULTY

I am grateful to Joshua Cohen, Charles Larmore, Michael McConnell, Richard Posner, Richard Ross, David Strauss, and Cass Sunstein for their comments on an earlier draft, and to Abner Mikva, Sara Nussbaum, Stephen Schulhofer, and Arnold Wolf for related discussions of the history of Judaism. For further clarification of my own views about religion, see my "Judaism and the Love of Reason," in *Among Sophia's Daughters: Reflections on Philosophy, Feminism, and Faith*, ed. Marya Bower and Ruth Groenhout (forthcoming).

1. The salient exceptions are John Stuart Mill and John Rawls (see his "The Idea of Public Reason Revisited," *University of Chicago Law Review* 64, 3 [1997]: 765–807).

2. For this reason, Reform and Reconstructionist Jews carefully avoid the masculine pronoun in referring to God, either replacing it by "you," changing third person to second, or simply repeating the word "God." Nor is this simply a revisionist ploy: many classic sources (for example, the central prayer "Adon Olam") depict God as without body, therefore without gender. For discussion of the history of Reform Judaism on issues of both feminism and cosmopolitanism, see my "Judaism and the Love of Reason."

3. My use of these terms follows that of John Rawls.

4. Mill's understanding of Calvinism is superficial; he does not understand, for example, that the absolute character of God's sovereignty strips earthly monarchs of their claim to absolute rule; thus Calvinism supported struggles for liberal republicanism in Holland, Scotland, and New England.

5. I believe judgments about polygamy should be highly contextual. In some circumstances, a woman's choice to enter a polygamous marriage should be seen as that, and respected. For example, I believe that the United States behaved unwisely, and on the basis of prejudice and superstition, in its assault on Mormon polygamy, in the face of evidence that Mormon women freely endorsed the system. In Kerala in South India, polygamous marriages for women have historically been one factor in women's attaining higher status and a better life quality than they enjoy in other regions. In the case of Hindu polygamy, however, which was so closely bound up with a more general denial of marital consent and with a denial to women of educational and employment opportunities, the state was probably correct in taking the step it took. It was understandable that the state allowed polygamy to remain legal for Muslims, given the more central place of polygamy in the Islamic tradition and the special sensitivity of minority rights; and yet in principle the change should not have been made in a way that discriminated among religions.

6. Two other changes introduced by the reforms—the abolition of child marriage and the granting to Hindu women of a right of divorce—were also attacked by Hindu leaders on free exercise grounds. In the case of divorce, one should not grant that a substantial burden has been applied. It is never a legitimate instance of free exercise to compel another person to obey a religious commandment against his or her will. The case of child marriage is more complicated, as is any case involving parents' control over the religious upbringing of young children. Either we should say that denying parents the right to marry off their young daughters without consent imposes no substantial burden on their free exercise, or we should grant that it does so, but insist (as with polygamy) that the state had a compelling interest in the change.

7. None of the reforms has been adequately enforced. Child marriage remains common in some regions; dowry giving is ubiquitous, as is the associated violence that the laws aimed to curtail; and the rate of polygamy among Hindus is exactly the same as among Muslims (both around 5.8 percent).

8. I understand these goals as a set of capabilities or opportunities, not actual functions: thus if religions teach that their members should not vote, or if a given religious order imposes on its members a vow of poverty, or silence, or urges strenuous fasting, these restrictions do not run afoul of my understanding of basic political principles, so long as the political conception continues to extend to all citizens the full menu of rights and opportunities, and the choice to enter the religious group is fully voluntary.

9. By this I mean just that, opportunity: i.e., jobs are open to women on an equal basis, women are not threatened or intimidated when they attempt to go out and work (as they often are in India), and the like. I do not mean that the state should promote female employment; indeed I think the state should make sure women really have a choice in this matter—for example, by taking the financial value of domestic labor into account when calculating settlement after divorce, a suggestion that is central to Okin's argument in *Justice, Gender, and the Family*.

SUSAN MOLLER OKIN
REPLY

Many thanks to Joshua Cohen and Cass Sunstein for their very helpful comments on earlier versions of both my essay and my reply, and to Elisabeth Hansot and David Tyack, for their support and inspiration as I embarked upon writing the reply.

1. For an extreme example of enculturation for servitude, see Elinor Burkett, "God Created Me to Be a Slave," *New York Times Magazine*, 12 October 1997, pp. 56-60. Burkett reports of Mauritania's ninety thousand slaves that "[t]he possibility of rebellion, like the possibility of a world made up entirely of free men and women, is inconceivable among people who have lost their collective memory of freedom" (p. 57). I shall discuss explanations of less extreme examples of indoctrination into subordinate status below.

2. See, for example, Susan Moller Okin, *Women in Western Political Thought* (Princeton: Princeton University Press, 1979) and *Justice, Gender, and the Family* (New York: Basic Books, 1989).

3. Susan Moller Okin, "Liberty and Welfare: Some Issues in Human Rights Theory," in *Human Rights*, ed. J. Roland Pennock and John W. Chapman, NOMOS XXIII (New York: New York University Press, 1981), pp. 230-56.

4. For a recent argument to this effect, see James Hamilton, *Channeling Violence* (Princeton: Princeton University Press, 1998).

5. The chairman of the religious council in Jerusalem, Rabbi Yizhak Ralbag, was recently quoted as resisting the inclusion of Orthodox women, as well as all non-Orthodox Jews, on the rabbinical councils that make many important rulings in Israel, because such inclusion "gives them legitimacy" ("Battle Looms in Israel over 'Mixed' Religious Councils," *New York Times*, 2 December 1998, A3). Of

course, there are many Jews in Israel and elsewhere who think more like Nussbaum than like this, but one cannot reasonably claim the stances of Jews at the antifeminist end of the spectrum as "defective historical practices" and the stances of those at the feminist end as "a more authentic [or orthodox] realization of Judaism."

6. See, for example, Abdullahi An-Na'im, *Toward an Islamic Reformation: Civil Liberties, Human Rights, and International Law* (Syracuse, NY: Syracuse University Press, 1990); Azizah al-Hibri, "Islam, Law and Custom: Redefining Muslim Women's Rights," *American University Journal of International Law and Policy* 12, 1 (1997): 1–44.

7. Of course, this was only her impression, but at least she, unlike Western feminists who defend polygamy as good for women, lives in the midst of many women in polygamous marriages and is more likely to know what they think.

8. Avishai Margalit, "Israel: The Rise of the Ultra-Orthodox," *New York Review of Books*, 9 November 1989, pp. 38–44.

9. For explanation of this point, see Nahid Toubia, *Female Genital Mutilation: A Call for Global Action* (New York: Rainb and Women, Ink., 1995), p. 9.

10. On adaptive preferences in general, see, for example, Jon Elster, *Sour Grapes: Studies in the Subversion of Rationality* (Paris: Maison des Sciences de l'Homme; Cambridge: Cambridge University Press, 1983), and Cass Sunstein, *Free Markets and Social Justice* (Oxford: Oxford University Press, 1997), chaps. 1–2. On such preferences and self-conceptions in women, see, for example, J. S. Mill, *The Subjection of Women* (1869; Indianapolis: Hackett, 1988), esp. pp. 14–17. On adaptive preferences specifically in the context of Third World women, see Amartya Sen, *Commodities and Capabilities* (Amsterdam: North-Holland, 1985), chap. 6 and appendix B; Uma Narayan, *Dislocating Cultures: Identities, Traditions, and Third World Feminism* (New York: Routledge, 1997), chap. 1; Martha Nussbaum, "Adaptive Preferences and Women's Options," in *Women and Human Development: The Capabilities Approach* (Cambridge: Cambridge University Press, forthcoming 2000), chap. 2.

11. For an excellent autobiographical account that mentions all of these factors, see Narayan, *Dislocating Cultures*, chap. 1, esp. pp. 6–12.

12. *Employment Division, Department of Human Resources v. Smith*, 404 U.S. 872 (1990).

13. See Nancy Rosenblum, *Membership and Morals: The Personal Uses of Pluralism in America* (Princeton: Princeton University Press, 1998), pp. 89–90, for discussion of how U.S. courts have been unwilling to make such judgments.

14. John Rawls, *Political Liberalism* (New York: Columbia University Press, 1993), pp. 199–200.

15. Recently, after I taught classes on Luther's and Calvin's ideas about religion and politics, a college senior who had attended a public high school in an affluent suburb came up to me and asked, "Did these people's ideas actually have much effect on anyone?"

CONTRIBUTORS

AZIZAH Y. AL-HIBRI is professor of law at the T. C. Williams School of Law, University of Richmond. She is also president and founder of KARAMAH: Muslim Women Lawyers for Human Rights, and author of many articles on Islamic jurisprudence.

ABDULLAHI AN-NA'IM is professor of law and fellow of the law and religion program at Emory University. He is author of *Toward an Islamic Reformation: Civil Liberties, Human Rights and International Law* (Syracuse) and editor of *Human Rights in Cross-Cultural Perspectives: Quest for Consensus* (Pennsylvania).

HOMI K. BHABHA is Chester D. Tripp Professor in the Humanities at the University of Chicago and visiting humanities professor at University College, London. His books include *Nation and Narration* and *The Location of Culture* (both Routledge).

JOSHUA COHEN is Sloan Professor of Political Science and professor of philosophy at MIT, and editor-in-chief of *Boston Review.* He is coauthor (with Joel Rogers) of *Associations and Democracy* (Verso).

SANDER L. GILMAN is Henry R. Luce Distinguished Service Professor of the Liberal Arts in Human Biology at the University of Chicago. His most recent book is *Creating Beauty to Cure the Soul: Race and Psychology in the Shaping of Aesthetic Surgery* (Duke).

JANET E. HALLEY is professor of law and Robert E. Paradise Faculty Scholar at Stanford University. Founding and executive editor of the *Yale Journal of Law and the Humanities*, she is author most recently of *Don't: A Reader's Guide to the Military's Anti-Gay Policy* (Duke).

BONNIE HONIG is professor of political science at Northwestern University and senior research fellow at the American Bar Foundation. She is author of *Political Theory and the Displacement of Politics* (Cornell) and editor of *Feminist Interpretations of Hannah Arendt* (Pennsylvania). Her latest book, *Democracy and the Politics of Foreignness* (Princeton), is forthcoming.

MATTHEW HOWARD is an editor and writer living in New York, and a contributing editor to *Boston Review.*

WILL KYMLICKA is professor in the philosophy department of Queen's University, in Kingston, Canada. He is author of *Multicultural Citizenship* (Oxford), which received the Ralph Bunche Award from the American Political Science Association. His edited books include *The Rights of Minority Cultures* (Oxford) and *Ethnicity and Group Rights* (NYU, coedited with Ian Shapiro).

MARTHA C. NUSSBAUM is Ernst Freund Distinguished Service Professor of Law and Ethics at the University of Chicago, appointed in the Law School, the Philosophy Department, and the Divinity School, with an associate appointment in Classics. Her books include *Cultivating Humanity: A Classical Defense of Reform in Liberal Education* (Harvard) and *Sex and Social Justice* (Oxford).

SUSAN MOLLER OKIN is Marta Weeks Professor of Ethics in Society and professor of political science at Stanford University. She is author of *Women in Western Political Thought* (Princeton) and *Justice, Gender, and the Family* (Basic).

BHIKHU PAREKH is professor of political theory at the University of Hull. His most recent books are *Gandhi* and *Rethinking Multiculturalism* (both Oxford).

KATHA POLLITT is a columnist for *The Nation* and author of *Reasonable Creatures: Essays on Women and Feminism* (Knopf).

ROBERT POST is Alexander F. and May T. Morrison Professor of Law at the University of California, Berkeley (Boalt Hall). He is author of *Constitutional Domains* (Harvard), editor of *Censorship and Silencing: Practices of Cultural Regulation* (Getty Museum), and coeditor of *Race and Representation: Affirmative Action* (Zone).

JOSEPH RAZ is professor of the philosophy of law at Oxford University and visiting professor at Columbia Law School. His most recent books are *The Morality of Freedom* (Oxford) and *Ethics in the Public Domain* (Clarendon). His new book *Reason, Value and Morality* will be published in 1999.

SASKIA SASSEN is professor of sociology at the University of Chicago. Among her recent books are *Losing Control? Sovereignty in an Age of Globalization* (Columbia) and *Globalization and Its Discontents* (The New Press).

CASS R. SUNSTEIN is Karl N. Llewellyn Distinguished Service Professor at the University of Chicago. He is author of many books, including *Free Markets and Social Justice*, *Legal Reasoning and Political Conflict* (both Oxford), and *One Case at a Time: Judicial Minimalism on the Supreme Court* (Harvard).

YAEL TAMIR is senior lecturer in political philosophy at Tel Aviv University. She is the chairperson of the board of the Association for Civil Rights in Israel and an active member of the Labor Party. Her books include *Liberal Nationalism* (Princeton) and *Democratic Education in a Multicultural State* (Blackwell).